THE HOLY SPIRIT

BASIC GUIDES TO CHRISTIAN THEOLOGY

THE HOLY SPIRIT

A Guide to Christian Theology

Veli-Matti Kärkkäinen

WESTMINSTER
JOHN KNOX PRESS
LOUISVILLE • KENTUCKY

First edition
Published by Westminster John Knox Press
Louisville, Kentucky

12 13 14 15 16 17 18 19 20 21—10 9 8 7 6 5 4 3 2 1

Book design by Sharon Adams
Cover design by Lisa Buckley

Library of Congress Cataloging-in-Publication Data
Kärkkäinen, Veli-Matti.
The Holy Spirit / Veli-Matti Kärkkäinen. — 1st ed.
    p. cm. — (Basic guides to theology series)
Includes bibliographical references (p.   ) and index.
ISBN 978-0-664-23593-2 (alk. paper)
1. Holy Spirit—History of doctrines. I. Title.
BT119.K37 2012
231'.3—dc23
                                              2012015853

♾ The paper used in this publication meets the minimum requirements of the American National Standard for Information Sciences—Permanence of Paper for Printed Library Materials, ANSI Z39.48-1992.

Contents

Preface

The writing process has been delightful and deeply gratifying. It has given me yet another opportunity to learn from and reflect on the rich tapestry of pneumatological lessons and insights. Providentially, this writing was preceded by another book on pneumatology, an anthology tracing readings on *Spirit and Salvation*[1] throughout Christian history. In preparation for that project, my last sabbatical from Fuller Theological Seminary gave me an opportunity to spend months and months in a careful reading and review of patristic, medieval, and Reformation writings by a host of authors. While keeping an eye on pneumatological and soteriological topics, I also indulged myself in a wider reading of the sources. That remarkable experience was still fresh in my mind as Dr. Donald McKim of Westminster John Knox Press approached me and suggested the current book project—to which I could only say an enthusiastic yes.

During the writing of this book I have had two opportunities to continue teaching special courses on pneumatology—experiences that I hope have helped me express my thoughts and interpretations in more transparent, faithful, and accurate ways. In the fall of 2009, I offered a graduate course in ecumenics at the University of Helsinki titled "Holy Spirit in Contemporary Theology," and in the winter of 2010 I conducted a doctoral seminar at Fuller Theological Seminary, Center of Advanced Theological Studies, on "Pneumatology: Contemporary Trends." To my students I offer most sincere thanks for engaging and exciting conversations.

To Susan Carlson Wood of Fuller Seminary's School of Theology faculty publications services I again owe a greater debt than I am able to express in words. Thank you for your highly professional and efficient editing of yet another work of mine. Sincere thanks also go to my Japanese doctoral student Naoki Inoue—currently in the process of writing a dissertation on Jürgen Moltmann's panentheistic pneumatology in dialogue with the Japanese Shintoistic view of the spirit—who checked all the references in the original sources.

Abbreviations

ANF   *The Ante-Nicene Fathers: Translations of the Writings of the Fathers Down to A.D. 325*. Ed. Alexander Roberts and James Donaldson. 10 vols. Buffalo, NY: Christian Literature, 1885–1896. Repr. Grand Rapids: Wm. B. Eerdmans Publishing Co., 1951–1956. http://www.ccel.org.

CCEL   Christian Classics Ethereal Library. http://www.ccel.org.

CD   Karl Barth, *Church Dogmatics*. 14 vols. Trans. and ed. G. W. Bromiley and T. F. Torrance. Edinburgh: T. & T. Clark, 1956–1977.

LW   *Luther's Works*. American edition. Ed. Jaroslav Pelikan and Helmut T. Lehman. 55 vols. Libronix Digital Library. Minneapolis: Fortress Press, 2002.

NPNF   *A Select Library of the Nicene and Post-Nicene Fathers of the Christian Church*. Ed. Philip Schaff et al. 14 vols. Buffalo, NY: Christian Literature, 1887–1894. Repr. Edinburgh: T. & T. Clark; Grand Rapids: Wm. B. Eerdmans Publishing Co., 1952–1956. *NPNF*[1] = First Series; *NPNF*[2] = Second Series. http://www.ccel.org.

ST   St. Thomas Aquinas, *Summa Theologica*. Trans. Fathers of the English Dominican Province. New York: Benziger Bros. ed., 1947, http://ccel.org.

TDNT   *Theological Dictionary of the New Testament*. Ed. G. Kittel and G. Friedrich. Trans. G. W. Bromiley. 10 vols. Grand Rapids: Wm. B. Eerdmans Publishing Co., 1964–1976.

Introduction

*Holy Spirit in Christian
Theology and Spirituality*

For a long time considered to be the stepchild of theology, pneumatology—the doctrine and spirituality of the Holy Spirit—has risen to the center of theological reflection and investigation. Never before in the history of Christian doctrine has there been so wide and varied interest in, and at times almost an enthusiasm over, the Holy Spirit. The Roman Catholic historian Elizabeth Dreyer, who has probed deeply into the medieval mystics' experiences of the Holy Spirit, offers an insightful observation:

> Renewed interest in the Holy Spirit is visible in at least three contexts: individual Christians who hunger for a deeper connection with God that is inclusive of all of life as well as the needs of the world; the church that seeks to renew itself through life-giving disciplines and a return to sources; and the formal inquiry of academic philosophy and theology. In effect, one can hear the petition, "Come Creator Spirit" on many lips these days.[1]

The Holy Spirit is not out there just for the sake of an academic study—as important as an adequate and respectful intellectual understanding of this topic is. As Dreyer goes on to say, "Many Christians desire to encounter a Holy Spirit who brings new life to their spirits in the concrete circumstances of their lives and who renews the face of the earth as we enter the third millennium."[2] The Holy Spirit is God, God's divine energy that permeates all life and everything in the cosmos. The Holy Spirit is also the most intimate "contact point" between the triune God and human beings. There is also a deep experience of the Holy Spirit—at times mystical, at times charismatic. The Holy Spirit manifests herself at times in the form of a rushing wind and at other times in the most subtle breeze. As we attempt to study the Spirit of God, we should also keep in mind the biblical reminder that we are also subjected to the deepest and most penetrating investigation of the Spirit of God: "The Spirit searches all things, even the deep things of God" (1 Cor. 2:10b).

It took a long time for Christian theology to come up with a precise and accurate account of the doctrine of the Holy Spirit. During the first centuries of Christian history, questions related to the Trinity and Christology occupied the best minds of the church. Not only was it more difficult to say something doctrinal about the Spirit than about the Father and Son, because by definition the Spirit is more subtle and less concrete a phenomenon, but there was also the biblical perception that the Holy Spirit never draws attention to herself but rather turns our attention to the Son and through the Son to the Father. On that basis, tradition at times speaks of the Spirit as the "Third Unknown." Other reasons for the slow doctrinal development of pneumatology may have to do with the naming of the Spirit as the "bond" of love between the Father and Son. While certainly this idea has both a biblical basis and theological validity, in the hands of less incisive theologians it may also turn into a nonpersonal conception of the Spirit. "Love" or "bond" doesn't have to be as "personal" as Father and Son.

Yet another reason for the junior role of the Spirit in the Trinitarian understanding of the Christian God may have to do with ecclesial concerns. As early as the charismatic revival movement beginning from the second century, Montanists all the way through Reformation "Enthusiasts" to modern-day Pentecostals started to claim the authority of the Spirit over human leaders of the church—or as it was often perceived, over the written Word of God. Thus, a need was felt to control the Spirit. The Eastern Orthodox Church in particular reminds us often that one important reason behind the lack of proper attention to the Holy Spirit has to do with the so-called *filioque* clause, which was added to the Nicene-Constantinopolitan Creed (381). This clause, which means literally "and from the Son," suggests the double derivation of the Spirit from both Father and Son (rather than from the Father alone, as the original creedal form said). This, in turn, might have led to the subordination of the Spirit to Christ, in other words, the placement of pneumatology under Christology.

In sum: a number of reasons contributed both to the slow development of the doctrine of the Holy Spirit and to the Spirit's occasionally receiving a minor role in Christian theology. Much of the early development of pneumatology—not unlike the doctrine of the Trinity and Christology—emerged out of painful encounters and rebuttals of heretical views. Oftentimes, it seemed to be easier for the church to say what they did not believe rather than state positively the orthodox position.

The purpose of this primer is to trace the narrative of the history and development of pneumatology, the doctrine of the Holy Spirit. After briefly looking at the biblical testimonies to the Spirit, the book discusses patristic, medieval, Reformation, and subsequent pneumatologies, culminating in a fairly comprehensive account of the contemporary state in current theology. In order to orient the reader to original sources, detailed documentation is offered in the notes. Nothing is more important and useful in the study of any theological topic than looking at the original writings out of which doctrines and interpretations emerge. While fully documented, the main text makes every effort to offer a *narrative*, a story of the experience, ministry, and doctrinal understanding of the Holy Spirit in Christian history and theology. The final chapter attempts a bird's-eye view of the ways that contemporary pneumatology differs from and builds on the heritage of tradition.

Chapter 1

Biblical Perspectives on the Spirit

The Bible presents the work of the Holy Spirit through symbols, images, metaphors, testimonies, and stories,[1] all of which appeal to the imagination as much as to rational discourse. The basic biblical terms *ruach*, in the Old Testament, and *pneuma*, in the New Testament carry similar ambiguity: "breath," "air," and "wind." Other metaphors used for the Spirit are fire, dove, and Paraclete. When doing pneumatology, or the doctrine of the Spirit, one should proceed cautiously and "softly" in order not to oversystematize or imprison the Spirit that "'blows where it chooses'" (John 3:8).

OLD TESTAMENT TESTIMONIES

The Old Testament[2] contains about one hundred references to the Spirit of God (Gen. 1:2: "a wind from God"; Isa. 11:2: "the spirit of the LORD . . . wisdom . . . counsel . . . knowledge"). From the beginning of the biblical narrative, the Spirit's role in creation as the principle of life comes to the fore. The same Spirit of God that participated in creation over the chaotic primal waters (Gen. 1:2) is the principle of human life as well (Gen. 2:7). This very same divine energy also sustains all life in the cosmos:

> When you [Yahweh] send forth your Spirit [*ruach*], they are created;
> and you renew the face of the ground.
>
> > (Ps. 104:30)

Similarly,

> when [Yahweh] take[s] away their breath [*ruach*], they die
> and return to their dust.
>
> > (Ps. 104:29)

The charismatic, empowering function of the divine *ruach* over the leaders of the people of Israel is narrated in historical books (Judg. 14:6; 1 Sam. 16:13). Part of the empowerment is bringing about specific capacities, such as those of the craftsman's skill (Exod. 31:3), the prophet's vision (Ezek. 3:12; 8:3; 11:1), or extraordinary wisdom (Dan. 6:3).

The prophetic books make the all-important link between the promised messiah and the Spirit. The messiah is the receiver of the Spirit and the Spirit's power (Isa. 11:1–8; 42:1–4; 49:1–6). The divine Spirit is given for the healing and restoration of the messianic people (Ezek. 18:31; Joel 2:28–32).

In the Wisdom literature, wisdom can be correlated or identified with the Word/Logos or with the Spirit (Prov. 8:22–31). This close connection between wisdom and the Spirit led early Christian theology—as will be noticed in the historical section—to sometimes confuse the roles of the Son and Spirit.

THE SPIRIT IN THE NEW TESTAMENT

The Synoptic Gospels of the New Testament[3] offer an authentic, thick Spirit-Christology.[4] Jesus' birth (Matt. 1:18–25; Luke 1:35), baptism (Matt. 3:17; Mark 1:11; Luke 3:22; John 1:33), testing in the wilderness (Matt. 4:1; Mark 1:12; Luke 4:1), and ministry with healings, exorcisms, and other miracles (Matt. 12:28; Luke 4:18; 11:20) are functions of the Spirit. Indicative of the eschatological ministry of the Spirit is Jesus' role as the baptizer in the Spirit (Matt. 3:11; Mark 13:11).

The transforming power of the Spirit is evident in the life of the early church. On the day of Pentecost, a powerful outpouring of the Spirit signaled the birth of the church (Acts 2:1–3) in fulfillment of the prophecy of Joel (2:28–29). The communities of the book of Acts received the Spirit with visible signs (4:31; 8:15–19; 10:44–47; 19:6), indeed, those signs were taken as the evidence of the work of God (8:12–25; 10:44–48; 19:1–7). Often at pivotal moments in the life of an individual or the church, the Holy Spirit was looked on as the source of an extraordinary power (9:17; 11:15–18; etc.). The Spirit empowered and directed the early church in her mission (8:29, 39; 10:19), often with the help of a special authority given to the leadership of the community (4:31; 5:1–10; 6:10; etc.).

Similarly to the Gospels, Paul[5] has a robust Spirit-Christology. Jesus was raised to new life by the Spirit (Rom. 1:4). The Spirit is the Spirit of Christ (Rom. 8:9; Gal. 4:6; Phil. 1:19). Therefore, it is only through the Spirit that the believer is able to confess that "Jesus is Lord" (1 Cor. 12:1–3); similarly, the *Abba* prayer of the children of God is the work of the Spirit (Rom. 8:15). To be "in Christ" and "in the Spirit" are virtually synonymous; therefore, the Spirit cannot be experienced apart from Christ (1 Cor. 12:3). At times the integral connection between the Spirit and Christ is so close that Paul speaks of Christ as "a life-giving Spirit" (1 Cor. 15:45). Along with the salvific functions, important for Paul is the charismatic endowment and gifting (1 Cor. 1:4–7; Gal. 3:5). Similarly, the Spirit works to give illumination and divine revelation in the face of affliction (1 Thess. 1:6; 1 Cor. 2:10–12; 2 Cor. 3:14–17). The eschatological orientation comes to the fore in that the new age has already broken into the old. The Spirit can be compared to an *arrabon,* a down payment of the coming glory (2 Cor. 1:22; 5:5; Eph. 1:13–14), or to the first installment of the believer's inheritance in the kingdom of God (Rom. 8:15–17; 14:17; 1 Cor. 6:9–11; 15:42–50; Gal. 4:6–7). In addition to charismatic, prophetic, and eschatological dimensions, a moral transformation is also part of the Pauline communities' experience of the Spirit (1 Cor. 6:9–11). There is a constant struggle between "Spirit" and "flesh" (Rom. 8:1–17; Gal. 5:16–26). Therefore, the believer has a responsibility to live her life in the power of the Spirit, "walking in the Spirit," being led by the Spirit (Rom. 8:4–6, 14; Gal. 5:16, 18, 25). To the extent that one advances, the fruit of the Spirit will become evident (Gal. 5:22–23).

The pneumatology of the Johannine literature is highly distinctive. That tradition makes use of the Old Testament's rich imagery related to the Spirit's life-giving power of water and breath: rebirth (John 3:5–8), spring of life (John 4:14; 6:63; 7:38–39), and new creation (John 20:22; cf. Gen. 2:7; Ezek. 37:9). The Johannine Epistles speak of anointing (1 John 2:20, 27), which is also a familiar Old Testament metaphor. The Johannine Jesus has been given the Spirit "without measure" (John 3:34). John also ties Jesus' gift of the Spirit more closely to Jesus' death (6:51–58, 62–63; 19:34). Perhaps the most distinctive feature of Johannine pneumatology is the naming of the Spirit as the "other Advocate [Paraclete]" (14:16), obviously implying that Jesus is the first (1 John 2:1). The term *parakletos* (from *para+kalein*) means "one called alongside to help," thus an advocate or defense attorney (John 14:26). In the book of Revelation, the Spirit plays a crucial role in inspiration and vision (1:10; 4:2; 14:13; 17:3; 19:10; 21:10; 22:17). The Apocalypse mentions "seven spirits" (1:4; 4:5) or the spirits of Jesus (3:1; 5:6), phrases typical of apocalyptic literature.

The Pastoral Letters seem quite shy about the manifested Spirit's ministry in the church. The Spirit's ministry is linked with gifting to the ministry and to inspiration of Scripture (2 Tim. 3:16; 1:7). Titus 3:5 connects the Holy Spirit with regeneration. While the book of Hebrews obviously knows about the charismatic life in the church (2:4), inspiration of Scripture (3:7; 9:8; 10:15) is a main theme. Significantly, the book also connects the Spirit with Christ's self-offering on the cross (9:14). The letters of Peter similarly connect the Spirit with inspiration (1 Pet. 1:11; 2 Pet. 1:21). First Peter (4:14) also makes the important connection between the Spirit and our suffering as Christians.

The New Testament also speaks of spirits vis-à-vis the Spirit of God. There is a battle between the kingdom of God and evil spirits (Mark 3:23–27 par.). Since there are both good spirits and bad, the church and individual Christians need to be able to discern the spirits (1 Cor. 12:10; 14:12; 2 Cor. 11:4).

THEOLOGICAL REFLECTIONS

What are some of the theological implications of the diverse biblical testimonies and experiences of the Holy Spirit? The first is the need to acknowledge and celebrate the diversity and plurality. While there is no denying some common themes, such as the Spirit's role in creation, inspiration, salvation, and empowerment and in relation to Christ, there is no attempt among the biblical writers to reduce the sphere or the ministry of the Spirit. The work of the Spirit has a gentle and subtle facet as well as the rushing-wind or stormy side. There is the silent, hidden side as well as the audible, visible, and tangible aspect; a salvific, soteriological ministry as well as gifting and empowering energies; and so forth.

Many find it highly interesting theologically that in the last part of the New Testament, the so-called Catholic Epistles, there is a shift from the charismatic and dynamic ministry and role of the Spirit to more "institutionalized" forms, such as the inspiration of Scripture and gifting to the ministry ("ordination"). Such a shift happened soon after the first centuries when church structures, established ministries such as the episcopacy, and the Christian canon were formed.

This development is intriguing in light of the later developments of pneumatology and church life. According to the New Testament scholar James D. G. Dunn, two ecclesiological "streams" have flowed alongside each other in the postbiblical era: one was charismatic and enthusiastic; the other, more conventional and traditional. The former might have been the "mainstream" during the first postbiblical century while the latter, the more established one, soon took the upper hand.[6] The Roman Catholic pneumatologist Yves Congar has argued that indeed in the beginning the church saw itself subject to the activity of the Spirit and filled with his gifts. As an example he mentions Clement of Rome, who said that the apostles "set out, filled with the assurance of the Holy Spirit, to proclaim the good news of the coming of the kingdom of heaven." Toward the end of the first century, Clement was also obliged to give rules for the church at Corinth as to the right use of charisms, implying that spiritual gifts were active at that time. Congar mentions Justin Martyr as an example: this late second-century Apologist claimed that prophecy and charismatic gifts still existed; in fact, it was believed that the charisms should accompany the church until the end.[7] Furthermore, according to Congar, there was no opposition yet between the growth of tradition (doctrinal development) and charisms, such as visions and warnings from the Spirit. Cyprian said of the Council of Carthage (252) that it had made decisions "under the inspiration of the Holy Spirit and according to the warnings given by the Lord in many visions." Cyprian himself (d. 258) is claimed to have had various kinds of visions from the Spirit.[8]

In sum, both in the biblical canon and in the ensuing early centuries, diversity and plurality were hallmarks of the experiences of the Spirit as well as doctrinal formulations. To these historical developments we turn next.

Chapter 2

Developing Pneumatological Doctrine in the Patristic Era

THE EARLIEST PNEUMATOLOGIES BEFORE NICEA

The Slow Growth of the Doctrine

The Spirit was first experienced in Christian life and community and only in the second movement reflected on in terms of theological categories: "Long before the Spirit was a theme of doctrine, He was a fact in the experience of the community."[1] The development of the doctrine of the Holy Spirit took place slowly as christological and Trinitarian debates stood at the forefront. Even the question of the divinity of the Spirit alongside the Father and Son, let alone the Spirit's place in the Trinity, took several centuries to be clarified. There was a "practical" need behind the doctrinal clarifications: the fact that the Spirit was being mentioned alongside the Father and Son in doxologies, prayers, and baptismal liturgies and that Christ's salvific benefits were believed to be conveyed to men and women by the Spirit seemed to require the full divine status of the third member of the Trinity. This belief is the essence of the ancient rule *lex orandi lex credendi* (the law of prayer [is or becomes] the law of believing).[2]

10

One of the reasons for the slow development of the doctrine also had to do with the nature of progressive revelation. This was the argument of Gregory of Nazianzus (or Nazianzen), one of the Cappadocian fathers, who were the greatest defenders and drafters of orthodox pneumatology:

> The Old Testament proclaimed the Father openly, and the Son more obscurely. The New manifested the Son, and suggested the Deity of the Spirit. Now the Spirit Himself dwells among us, and supplies us with a clearer demonstration of Himself. For it was not safe, when the Godhead of the Father was not yet acknowledged, plainly to proclaim the Son; nor when that of the Son was not yet received to burden us further (if I may use so bold an expression) with the Holy Ghost; lest perhaps people might, like men loaded with food beyond their strength, and presenting eyes as yet too weak to bear it to the sun's light, risk the loss even of that which was within the reach of their powers; but that by gradual additions, and, as David says, Goings up, and advances and progress from glory to glory, the Light of the Trinity might shine upon the more illuminated. For this reason it was, I think, that He *gradually* came to dwell in the Disciples, measuring Himself out to them according to their capacity to receive Him, at the beginning of the Gospel, after the Passion, after the Ascension, making perfect their powers, being breathed upon them, and appearing in fiery tongues. And indeed it is by little and little that He is declared by Jesus, as you will learn for yourself if you will read more carefully. I will ask the Father, He says, and He will send you another Comforter, even the spirit of Truth.[3]

The Apostolic Fathers, the first postbiblical teachers, claimed their teaching came from the apostles. Less innovative and all about faithfulness in the transmission of the apostolic tradition, they did not offer any sophisticated doctrinal pronouncements about the Spirit but rather stayed, in keeping with the New Testament testimonies, at the economic level (that is, concerned with the Spirit's role in salvation). Illustrative of the lack of sophistication of terminology is the often vague and undefined usage of the term "Spirit," which led at times to the confusion between the Son (Word) and Spirit.[4] As long as the Spirit was not differentiated from the Son as a separate hypostatic[5] entity, it was difficult to say if the Spirit was the power or influence of the Father (filling or empowering the Son) or something less than a person.

Well until the end of the third Christian century, confusion remained about the mutual relationship of and distinction between the Son and Spirit. The reasons were many, in addition to those mentioned above, namely, the church fathers' focus on the Spirit's activity in the order of salvation (the economic level), the lack of New Testament clarity about the relations between Trinitarian members, the apparent parallelism in the Old Testament between Word and Spirit,[6] and so forth. The second-century writing *2 Clement* is a case in point: the proper distinction between Son and Spirit is confused in sayings such as the following, which speaks of those who abuse flesh: "Such a one then shall not partake of the spirit, which is Christ."[7] Other examples come from *The Shepherd of Hermas*: at times, there is the blurring of the distinction between Son and Spirit, and in one instance even a conflation of the two with the saying that the "Spirit is the Son of God."[8] The famous Apologist Justin Martyr opined, "It is wrong, therefore, to understand the Spirit and the power of God as anything else than the Word, who is also the first-born of God."[9] His colleague Athenagoras presented a view of the Spirit strongly emanationist—"an effluence of God, flowing from Him, and returning back again like a beam of the sun"[10]—that has a hard time in accounting for the full personality of the Spirit.

The Trinitarian canons are still not fixed even in later second-century theologians such as Theophilus of Antioch and Irenaeus. Both define the Trinity in terms of God, Word, and Wisdom.[11] Theophilus even equated the Spirit with the Word, while Irenaeus equated it with Wisdom![12] Because of the lack of confession of the full deity of the Spirit, there were times when the Spirit was ranked as the "third" member in the Divine Society.[13]

Pneumatological Themes and Experiences

In order to get a feel of the earliest postbiblical pneumatologies and experiences of the Spirit, it is instructive to look at some defining theological topics and themes related to the ministry of the Spirit. The anonymous second-century *First Epistle to the Corinthians*[14] contains a number of references to the inspiration of the Scriptures by the Spirit, which are "the true utterances of the Holy Spirit."[15] The Holy Spirit was instrumental in the preaching of the apostles and the establishment of the first Christian communities.[16] Alongside the doctrine of the Scripture, early theologians started making links between the Spirit and the church. According to Ignatius, the bishop of Antioch, it was none other than the Holy Spirit who declared leading ecclesiological rules such as obedience to the bishop, the need for holiness, and the need for unity.[17]

For the second-century Apologists, who were always in search of bridges between Christian faith and pagan philosophies, pneumatology, alongside Christology, offered great resources. Tatian found such a bridge in his clever pneumatological account of theological anthropology that focused on the immortality of the soul. In his *Address to the Greeks*, in a section titled "The Theory of the Soul's Immortality," he contends that only in union with the Divine Spirit can a mortal human person share in the immortality of God.[18]

Perhaps because prophetic, mystical, and other spiritual experiences were quite common at the time—as, for example, narrated in *The Shepherd of Hermas*,[19] a mid-second-century document that also includes transportations and visions in the Spirit—a need arose to create criteria for the discernment of the Spirit. Since the Spirit was looked on as the divine guide in the church, not every spirit should be heeded; thus the need for spiritual discernment. The earliest Christian manual, *The Didache*, also known as the *Teaching of the Twelve Apostles*, written in the early second century, gives this advice:

> While a prophet is making ecstatic utterances, you must not test or examine him. For "every sin will be forgiven," but this sin "will not be forgiven." However, not everybody making ecstatic utterances is a prophet, but only if he behaves like the Lord. It is by their conduct that the false prophet and the [true] prophet can be distinguished. For instance, if a prophet marks out a table in the Spirit, he must not eat from it. If he does, he is a false prophet. Again, every prophet who teaches the truth but fails to practice what he preaches is a false prophet. . . . But if someone says in the Spirit, "Give me money, or something else," you must not heed him. However, if he tells you to give for others in need, no one must condemn him.[20]

Similarly *The Shepherd of Hermas*[21] encourages Christians to "try the man who has the Divine Spirit by his life," whether he possess the qualities of a sanctified person and behaves appropriately or not. At the same time, it points out the need not to grieve the Spirit; that may happen for example because of doubt.[22]

These kinds of advice were necessary to tackle the most serious ecclesiological and pneumatological challenge during the patristic era, namely, the second-century Montanist movement. That movement emerged around AD 160–170 around the Phrygian Pentapolis area, in what is modern Turkey. While there are various, even contradictory assessments of Montanism, the overall evaluation is that it arose from a false spirit and held an erroneous pneumatology. Typical charges include undermining the authority of the apostles and church hierarchy as well as following evil lifestyles.[23] Hippolytus, among others, criticized Montanus and the two accompanying women, Priscilla and Maximilla, for creating "novelties," heretical views concerning the Paraclete, or Holy Spirit, as well as the doctrine of the Trinity (with reference to Noetus, the modalist).[24] The bishop of Rome was also concerned about the rapid spread of this Montanist heresy.[25]

Allegedly a lawyer by training, the North African theologian Tertullian—who was instrumental in doctrinal developments as well, coining such key terms as *persona* and *trinitas*—earlier in his life was intimately related to Montanism. While leaving behind this movement and properly critiquing it, Tertullian is claimed to have written a treatise on ecstasy originally consisting of six books, to which a seventh was added, refuting the charges of Apollonius, the major critic of Montanus. Unfortunately, this writing, *De Ecstasi*, has not survived. Since chronology and biographical details of Tertullian's life are poorly known, there is a debate among the scholars as to which writings of his, if any, betray Montanist biases. His *On Baptism*, a major pneumatological treasure as well, is a case in point.[26] Far from being merely an academic and historical question, this question has everything to do with the judgment on the shape and orientations of early Christian pneumatology.

A contemporary writing titled *The Passion of the Holy Martyrs Perpetua and Felicitas*,[27] a hagiography (a biography of a holy person) that offers a fascinating description of an eschatologically loaded charismatic spirituality similar to that of Montanism, is another indication of the appeal of such mystical and charismatic spirituality. Interestingly enough, the writing also has a relationship to Tertullian. Again, historical details, unfortunately, are unknown. While few if any contemporary scholars believe the narrative itself comes from the pen of Tertullian, it might be possible that he was a kind of editor or at least transmitter of the story.[28]

Toward the Deity of the Spirit in the Trinity

While the full deity of the Spirit was yet to be universally established in the Nicene-Constantinopolitan Creed (381), the third-century fathers made significant contributions in that direction. Indicative of the superb difficulties that faced even the ablest fathers in establishing the full deity and equality of the Spirit in the Trinity is Origen's strange idea of the derivation of the Spirit from the Logos. According to this great theologian, from the premise that the Holy Spirit is created (!) we "must necessarily assume that the Holy Spirit was made through the Logos, the Logos accordingly being older than he."[29] This statement is of course unorthodox and unsatisfactory in more than one way, and Origen had opportunities to correct himself later; yet these kinds of examples help us better understand the difficulty of the task at that time.

From the biblical statements about the Holy Spirit and his work, Origen[30] and others found a more solid basis for the emerging affirmation of the divinity of the Spirit. Throughout the patristic writings, theology about the nature and status of the Spirit was derived from the works of the Spirit (as well as that of Father and Son) in creation and salvation. For Origen the fact that it was impossible to think of regeneration or deification (the Eastern Church's designation for salvation) apart from the full cooperation of the Father, Son, and Spirit pushed the doctrinal reflections toward the idea of the full equality of the three.[31]

The subordination of the Spirit to the Father—and at times even to the Son, as explained above—was a general idea among the Fathers. Famous here is Irenaeus's idea of the Word and Spirit as the "two hands" of God bringing about creation.[32] Similarly, the dual role of the Son and Spirit comes to the fore in salvation; Irenaeus formulates his soteriology in terms of the Eastern concept of *theosis*, deification: In the last days, the Son "was made a man among men, that He might join the end to the beginning, that is, man to God . . . in order that man, having embraced the Spirit of God, might pass into the glory of the Father."[33] Whereas in later theology, especially in the Christian West, soteriology came to be linked predominantly with Christology, Irenaeus displays a healthy balance between christological and pneumatological understandings of salvation:

> Since the Lord thus has redeemed us through His own blood, giving His soul for our souls, and His flesh for our flesh, and has also poured out the Spirit of the Father for the union and communion of God and man, imparting indeed God to men by means of the Spirit, and, on the other hand, attaching man to God by His own incarnation, and bestowing upon us at His coming immortality durably and truly, by means of communion with God,—all the doctrines of the heretics fall to ruin.[34]

A major architect in the development of Trinitarian doctrine, including pneumatology, was Tertullian, who, as mentioned above, coined several key terms. According to this North African theologian, Trinity is the doctrine that distinguishes Christian faith from Judaism[35]—and it occupies the major part of one of his greatest works, *Against Praxeas*, a refutation of a heretic who was claimed to teach modalism (according to which Father, Son, and Spirit only stand for names or "modes" rather than "persons"). Tertullian based the distinctions among Father, Son, and Spirit on their inner relationships. Based on the Paraclete passages in John 14, Tertullian suggested that the Son distinguished both the Father and Spirit from himself.[36] Similarly, Origen affirmed that Jesus' referring to the Father and the Paraclete as distinct from himself implies the existence of three persons and one shared substance or entity.[37]

That said, at times the stress on the integral relationship between the Spirit and the Word in Tertullian borders on the blurring of the hypostatic distinction between the two. Taking his cue from Psalm 33:6, which speaks of the creation of the heavens and earth by the Word and Spirit, Tertullian surmises that "the Spirit (or Divine Nature) . . . was in the Word." He continues, "Do you then . . . grant that the Word is a certain substance, constructed by the Spirit and the communication of Wisdom? Certainly I do."[38] or "But the Word was formed by the Spirit, and (if I may so express myself) the Spirit is the body of the Word."[39]

While distinguished from one another, the Trinitarian persons also share unity, which later creedal tradition refers to as *homoousios* (consubstantial). Tertullian surmised that the Johannine saying of Jesus "'I and the Father are one'" means that Father and Son are of "one substance"[40] and that this denotes an identity of substance rather than numerical unity.[41] By extension, the Son and Spirit are of the same substance with the Father.[42] Thus, we can speak of God's one "substance" and three distinct yet undivided "persons."[43] Technically this is what the Western church's semicanonized way of expressing its faith in the Trinity says: "one substance in three persons" (*una substantia, tres personae*). Materially, this formulation leads to the full establishment of the deity of the Spirit. Among the Greek fathers, Origen finally came to this idea—after much vacillation, as reported above—when he affirmed that "nothing in the Trinity can be called greater or less, since the fountain of divinity alone contains all things by His word and reason, and by the Spirit of His mouth sanctifies all things."[44]

While conceptually innovative and intellectually rigorous, Tertullian was also fond of metaphors and symbols in his exposition of theology, in this case drawn from nature. While these metaphors properly establish the necessary interconnectedness of the Trinitarian members, they also tend to strengthen the then prevailing subordinationist notion of the Spirit:

> The Word, therefore, is both always in the Father. . . . For God sent forth the Word, as the Paraclete also declares, just as the root puts forth the

tree, and the fountain the river, and the sun the ray. . . . I should not hesi-
tate, indeed, to call the tree the son or offspring of the root, and the river
of the fountain, and the ray of the sun; because every original source is a
parent, and everything which issues from the origin is an offspring. . . .
But still the tree is not severed from the root, nor the river from the fountain, nor the ray from the sun; nor, indeed, is the Word separated from
God. Following, therefore, the form of these analogies, I confess that I
call God and His Word—the Father and His Son—*two*. For the root and
the tree are distinctly two things, but correlatively joined; the fountain
and the river are also two forms, but indivisible; so likewise the sun and
the ray are two forms, but coherent ones. . . . Now the Spirit indeed is
third from God and the Son; just as the fruit of the tree is third from the
root, or as the stream out of the river is third from the fountain, or as the
apex of the ray is third from the sun.[45]

The Spirit's Work and Ministry

Doctrinal clarification among the third-century fathers, particularly with regard
to the Spirit's deity, proceeded with profound reflection on the various works
and ministries of the Spirit. Again, we have to remind ourselves of the ancient
rule *lex orandi, lex credendi*; the basis for doctrinal insights was always the "economy" of the Spirit.

Building on the earlier traditions, third-century fathers developed several aspects
of ecclesiology from a pneumatological perspective. For Irenaeus, the presence of the
Spirit is the church-constitutive act: "For where the Church is, there is the Spirit of
God; and where the Spirit of God is, there is the Church, and every kind of grace;
but the Spirit is truth."[46] This same Spirit brings life and renewal to the church in a
way analogous to the creation of the first human being as a result of Yahweh's breathing into Adam's nostrils.[47] For Hippolytus, the presbyter in Rome and Irenaeus's
pupil, the Holy Spirit guaranteed the faithful transmission of Christian tradition in
the service of which the episcopal office also functioned.[48] The episcopal office was
not seen in any way contrasted with the ministry of the Spirit; even the consecration
to the office was a charismatic event.[49] If ministry and episcopacy are pneumatologically grounded, so are also the sacraments, as explained by Tertullian, who surmised
that similarly to the way the Spirit of God hovered over the primal waters, the Spirit
also lingers over the baptismal waters.[50] He saw even in the rite itself, namely, in
the laying on of the hand on the baptized person, an "invoking and inviting [of]
the Holy Spirit through benediction."[51] Cyprian highlighted the Spirit's ministry
in baptism with regard to our sanctification and purification,[52] and Clement of
Alexandria, often named the first Alexandrian theologian, saw "illumination, and
perfection, and washing" as results of the Spirit's work in water baptism.[53] Similarly,
several third-century theologians also spoke of the sacrament of the Eucharist in
pneumatological terms. Clement's allegorical explanation of the salvific meaning of
Christ's blood at the Eucharist is a case in point. In the background of this exposition
is also a robust Spirit-Christology:

And the blood of the Lord is twofold. For there is the blood of His flesh, by which we are redeemed from corruption; and the spiritual, that by which we are anointed. And to drink the blood of Jesus, is to become partaker of the Lord's immortality; the Spirit being the energetic principle of the Word, as blood is of flesh. Accordingly, as wine is blended with water, so is the Spirit with man. And the one, the mixture of wine and water, nourishes to faith; while the other, the Spirit, conducts to immortality. And the mixture of both—of the water and of the Word—is called Eucharist, renowned and glorious grace; and they who by faith partake of it are sanctified both in body and soul.[54]

While episcopacy and church structures were well in place, the third-century church was no stranger to charismatic manifestations, such as speaking in tongues.[55] Even such a conservative leader as Hippolytus, who vehemently opposed the Montanist movement, makes a reference in *The Apostolic Tradition* to "On Charismatic Gifts," a work lost to us that allegedly contained teaching about the use of charismatic gifts.[56] The dynamism of the charismatic life is well illustrated in Tertullian's[57] description of the charismatic element evident in the life of a lady believer:

> For, seeing that we acknowledge spiritual *charismata*, or gifts, we too have merited the attainment of the prophetic gift, although coming after John (the Baptist). We have now amongst us a sister whose lot it has been to be favoured with sundry gifts of revelation, which she experiences in the Spirit by ecstatic vision amidst the sacred rites of the Lord's day in the church: she converses with angels, and sometimes even with the Lord; she both sees and hears mysterious communications; some men's hearts she understands, and to them who are in need she distributes remedies. Whether it be in the reading of Scriptures, or in the chanting of psalms, or in the preaching of sermons, or in the offering up of prayers, in all these religious services matter and opportunity are afforded to her of seeing visions. It may possibly have happened to us, whilst this sister of ours was rapt in the Spirit, that we had discoursed in some ineffable way about the soul.[58]

Tertullian not only acknowledges the role and importance of charisms but indeed challenges his opponent Marcion to show off similar gifts as evidence of the genuine nature of his faith.[59] Origen used the same method in his main apologetic work, his multivolume *Against Celsus*, a defense of the Christian faith in opposition to a Greek philosopher named Celsus. Origen challenges Celsus to show off the apostolic "manifestation of the Spirit and of power," such as prophecy and "signs and wonders" in his defense.[60]

The unity of the church—a key concern for early theologians as illustrated wonderfully in Cyprian's *On the Unity of the Church*—while based on the unity among the Trinitarian members,[61] also has a distinctively pneumatological basis with reference to the gentle dovelike nature of the Spirit.[62]

THE EASTERN FATHERS ON PNEUMATOLOGY

Heretics in View

The fourth-century Greek-speaking theologians who made lasting contributions to pneumatology came mainly from Alexandria, the major center of theological reflection along with Antioch.[63] Setting their views against pneumatological heretical opinions such as those of the *Tropicii* (Tropici), a group that was not willing to give the same divine status to the Spirit as to the Son, Athanasius wrote his *Letters to Serapion concerning the Holy Spirit* (AD 355–60).[64] The first part of the letter scrutinizes scriptural passages used by the opponents in their denial of the Spirit's divinity (1.1–14). The second part (1.15–33) then refutes the main arguments of the *Tropicii*, one of which is that the Spirit is a "son" (or "brother") of the Son (1.15).

The Cappadocians wrote against the *Pneumatomachoi*, the fighters of the Spirit who undermined the Nicean orthodoxy and thus echoed Arian misgivings about the equality of the Son with the Father. Basil the Great's *On the Holy Spirit* (AD 376) had as its main target these heretics. Heresy was not a small thing for these defenders of emerging orthodoxy: those who opposed the equality of the Spirit in the Trinity were not only in error but also "transgressors."[65] Consequently, the best tools available should be employed to combat the errors. Basil, who had received training in rhetoric and logic, offers a highly sophisticated and detailed rebuttal of the arguments set forth by the *Pneumatomachoi*, analyzing the pronouns used both in the beginning (2.4–5.12) and the end of the treatise (25.58–27.68). Basil also lists attributes of the Spirit that belong to deity, such as preexistence.[66] While focusing on the Holy Spirit, Basil's treatise is indeed a powerful Trinitarian exposition in which the status of the Son in relation to the Father is dealt with extensively.[67] St. Basil's brother Gregory, the Bishop of Nyssa, penned his *On the Holy Trinity of the Godhead of the Holy Spirit to Eustathius* and *On the Holy Spirit against the Followers of Macedonius* (AD 381), in which he defends the Cappadocian conviction of the equality of the Spirit in the Trinity against Macedonius, a sectarian leader, deposed from the See of Constantinople in AD 360. With Arian and Eunomian tendencies, Macedonius compromised the Spirit's divinity and full equality with the Father. Against those heresies, Gregory mounts evidence hard to dismiss:

> The Holy Spirit is . . . because of qualities that are essentially holy, that which the Father, essentially Holy, is; and such as the Only-begotten is, such is the Holy Spirit; then, again, He is so by virtue of life-giving, of imperishability, of unvariableness, of everlastingness, of justice, of wisdom, of rectitude, of sovereignty, of goodness, of power, of capacity to give all good things, and above them all life itself, and by being everywhere, being present in each, filling the earth, residing in the heavens, shed abroad upon supernatural Powers, filling all things.[68]

Yet another Cappadocian father, Gregory of Nazianzus—one of the three persons in the Eastern Church called "theologians" along with St. John the Evangelist and Symeon the New Theologian—devotes the fifth sermon in his *The Theological Orations* to the Holy Spirit. A one-time bishop and presider of the Council of Constantinople for a while, he clarifies the doctrine of the Spirit vis-à-vis heretical views of Arians, Eunomians, and others who contested orthodoxy.[69] As with his colleagues, the ancient rule *lex orandi, lex credendi* still serves as a key tool in defending the deity of the Spirit: "For if He is not to be worshipped, how can He deify me by Baptism? But if He is to be worshipped, surely He is an Object of adoration, and if an Object of adoration He must be God."[70]

The Establishment of the Divinity and Equality of the Spirit

One of Basil's lasting contributions—an idea contested by his opponents—is the introduction of a new doxological formula: "Glory to the Father with the Son together with the Holy Spirit" replacing the older one, "Glory to the Father through the Son in the Holy Spirit." On this basis, Basil contended, it was appropriate to glorify the Spirit along with the Father and Son.[71] While he acknowledged that this new phrase was considered a novelty and against the tradition,[72] Basil still believed it was in keeping with biblical teaching and tradition.

Everywhere, the Greek fathers affirmed boldly the equality of the Spirit with the Son.[73] The Archbishop of Jerusalem, Cyril, in his teaching manual *Catechetical Lectures*, urged Christians to regard the Spirit in the same way as the Father and Son.[74] Athanasius insisted that the Spirit is in Christ as the Son is in the Father,[75] and he also insisted on the indivisibility of the Trinity as another proof of the equal status of the Spirit.[76] The force of the logic itself seemed to speak against any notion of the Spirit as creature: if there ever was time when the Father was not—meaning he was not eternal because there then was a beginning—then the Son would not be eternal either, and by derivation the Spirit.[77] But that would of course compromise all notions of orthodox doctrine of God. In other words, brushed away is the notion of the *Tropicii* that the Spirit would be a creature. Similarly to Arian heresy in Christology, that would lead to pneumatological heresy.[78] Kelly summarizes succinctly Athanasius's contribution in response to Arians and others who denied the deity of the Spirit. He writes that Athanasius's teaching[79]

> is that the Spirit is fully divine, consubstantial with the Father and the Son. . . . The Spirit "belongs to and is one with the Godhead Which is the Triad." . . . The Spirit comes from God, bestows sanctification and life, and is immutable, omnipresent and unique. . . . The Triad is eternal, homogenous and indivisible, and . . . since the Spirit is a member of it He must therefore be consubstantial with Father and Son. . . . He belongs in essence to the Son exactly as the Son does to the Father.

As much as the Cappadocians labored in defense of the deity and equality of the Spirit, in the final analysis they never came to call the Spirit "God," since the

Bible does not do so. The closest St. Basil comes to affirming this is to say "that the Holy Spirit partakes of the fullness of divinity."[80] Basil also calls the Spirit "Lord," based on biblical teaching.[81]

While theologically and conceptually sophisticated, these Eastern theologians always went back to and consulted the biblical canon for their views of the Spirit. They did not want to establish any opinion concerning the Spirit without biblical warrant.[82] At the same time, there was a high regard of the developing Christian tradition, particularly the teaching of the Fathers.[83] Similarly to their predecessors, these spiritual teachers also saw indications of the Trinity and the Spirit in the created order, both in the human being—"The threefold Names are sown in a threefold way, in the spirit and in the soul and in the body, as in the mystery"[84]—and nature: "Lo, there is a similitude between the sun and the Father, the radiance and the Son, the heat and the Holy Ghost; and though it be one, a trinity is beheld in it!"[85] Athanasius compared the Father to fountain, the Son to river, and our reception of the Spirit to drinking this water, as Paul says in 1 Corinthians 12:13.

Reflecting biblical teaching, both in the Gospels and Pauline literature, the integral link between the Spirit and Christ was a leading theme: "When we are given to drink of the Spirit, we drink Christ" (with appeal to 1 Cor. 10:4).[86] The cooperation in creation and resurrection similarly speaks of the close link between the Son and Spirit.[87] This Spirit-Christology is an important theme in Eastern pneumatology at large. Basil's brother, Gregory of Nyssa, explains this in a most dramatic way:

> For as between the body's surface and the liquid of the oil nothing intervening can be detected, either in reason or in perception, so inseparable is the union of the Spirit with the Son; and the result is that whosoever is to touch the Son by faith must needs first encounter the oil in the very act of touching; there is not a part of Him devoid of the Holy Spirit. Therefore belief in the Lordship of the Son arises in those who entertain it, by means of the Holy Ghost; on all sides the Holy Ghost is met by those who by faith approach the Son. If, then, the Son is essentially a King, and the Holy Spirit is that dignity of Kingship which anoints the Son, what deprivation of this Kingship, in its essence and comparing it with itself, can be imagined?[88]

Not only is the Spirit linked with Christ, the Greek fathers also never lose sight of the Trinitarian ramifications of pneumatology. One of the many ways this comes to the fore is in the "rule of knowledge," according to which the Spirit is the first "contact" point for us with the Trinity: from the Spirit, through the Christ, we ascend to the knowledge of the Father: "Thus the way of the knowledge of God lies from One Spirit through the One Son to the One Father, and conversely the natural Goodness and the inherent Holiness and the royal Dignity extend from the Father through the Only-begotten to the Spirit."[89]

The Ministry of the Spirit

Establishing the deity and equality of the Spirit in the Trinity was not the only—
nor always the primary—task of the fourth-century Greek fathers. As did their
predecessors, these teachers also continued reflecting on the nature and ministry
of the Spirit, building on biblical and Christian traditions. One of the valuable
lessons about the nature of the Spirit that did not go unnoticed is the Spirit's
gentleness and meekness.[90]

Everywhere in the writings of the Eastern fathers the Holy Spirit is connected
with the salvific vision of *theosis*, deification. The union between the human
being and God is the function of the Holy Spirit; that work is yet another indication of the divinity of the Spirit: a creature could never help other creatures to
participate in the divine nature.[91] Eastern Father's litany of the salvific works of
the Spirit is illustrative:

> The Holy Ghost, having His subsistence of God, the fount of holi-
> ness, power that gives life, grace that maketh perfect, through Whom
> man is adopted, and the mortal made immortal, conjoined with Father
> and Son in all things in glory and eternity, in power and kingdom, in
> sovereignty and godhead; as is testified by the tradition of the baptism
> of salvation.[92]

> Through the Holy Spirit comes our restoration to paradise, our ascen-
> sion into the kingdom of heaven, our return to the adoption of sons, our
> liberty to call God our Father, our being made partakers of the grace of
> Christ, our being called children of light, our sharing in eternal glory,
> and, in a word, our being brought into a state of all "fulness of blessing,"
> both in this world and in the world to come, of all the good gifts that are
> in store for us, by promise hereof, through faith, beholding the reflec-
> tion of their grace as though they were already present, we await the full
> enjoyment.[93]

Cyril urged baptismal candidates—who were "about to be presented to God
before tens of thousands of the Angelic Hosts"—to be assured of the sealing by
the Holy Spirit, of spiritual grace communicated via the waters sanctified by the
Spirit, and of holiness thus imparted.[94] Jesus' baptism in the Jordan with the
reception of the Holy Spirit was seen as the biblical precedent and pattern for
this pneumatological view of the sacrament of water baptism.[95]

One of the distinctive emphases of many Eastern fathers, particularly of the
so-called desert fathers (such as Pseudo-Macarius of Egypt, who not only is
highly venerated by the Catholic tradition but whose homilies were translated
by John Wesley) is the stress on spiritual exercises as a means of acquiring the
Spirit. This notion of *synergia*, human-divine cooperation, is in keeping with the
soteriology of the Christian East. Differently from the West, this synergy was
never considered as a merit but rather a proper response to the gracious invita-
tion of God. Pseudo-Macarius thus teaches,

> We have offered . . . examples from Holy Scripture to show that the power
> of divine grace is in man and the gift of the Holy Spirit which is given to
> the faithful soul comes forth with much contention, with much endurance,
> patience, trials, and testings. . . . He also receives the full adoption of the
> Spirit, which is always a mystery, along with spiritual riches and wisdom
> which are not of this world, of which true Christians are made participa-
> tors. . . . But one cannot possess his soul and the love of the heavenly Spirit
> unless he cuts himself off from all the things of this world and surrenders
> himself to seek the love of Christ.[96]

The desert fathers also speak of the necessity for a Spirit-filled life to keep
the commandments, maintain purity, renounce all worldly things, persevere
constantly in prayer as well as excel in all good work.[97] Such a person is fit for
fighting "evil spirits" and quenching "the fiery darts of the wicked one."[98] It is
only Christians "rich in the Holy Spirit" who

> truly possess the fellowship of the Spirit within themselves. And when they
> speak words of truth or deliver any spiritual conference and wish to edify
> persons, they speak out of the same wealth and treasure which indwells
> within them and out of this they edify persons who listen to their spiri-
> tual discourses. And they do not fear lest they run short since they possess
> within themselves the heavenly treasure of goodness from which they draw
> to feed those who hunger for spiritual food.[99]

While the charismatic vitality seems to be tamed down and become more
sporadic after the earliest centuries, it was not unknown to fourth-century
fathers. While historical questions, including that of authorship of the *Life
of Antony* (a hagiography of a monk by the name Antony) are scarce, and
while we do not know if Athanasius wrote it, its linkage with this great
teacher should not be easily dismissed. This work discusses widely the role
of evil spirits and demons and how they could be combated. Various types
of miracles, including healings, are attributed to Antony as well.[100] Testimonies of miraculous healings and other miracles were recorded by Gregory
of Nazianzus. In a moving passage in a funeral sermon preached in the
presence of St. Basil on the occasion of his father's death, Gregory talks
about three significant events in his and his family's life in which the Spirit
intervened, saving and protecting. He tells vividly about the miraculous
healings of his father and then his mother and finally about his own survival
in a storm.[101]

Similarly to the charismatic dimension of the Christian life, the eschatological expectation of the imminent return of Christ seemed to disappear
gradually over the centuries. A few theologians, such as the Cappadocian Basil,
however, reminded their audience of the integral link between the Spirit and
eschatology. According to Basil, even in the final revelation of Christ the Spirit
is not inactive; rather, the Spirit "will be present with Him" helping execute
the final acts of the bringer of the kingdom of God, including judgment and
rewards.[102]

THE HOLY SPIRIT
IN THE TEACHING OF THE LATIN FATHERS

Biblical Teaching on the Spirit

In keeping with precedent, biblical testimonies and teaching were consulted by all the Latin fathers when reflecting on the Trinity and the Spirit. The former lawyer and governor, then bishop of Milan (who took that position only eight days after his baptism), St. Ambrose found pneumatological lessons in the allegorical exposition of the Old Testament. This is evident in his three-volume *Of the Holy Spirit*, which, indeed, is nothing else than a biblical exposition. The first two volumes concentrate on the Old Testament. Symbols such as water and river illustrate the nature and work of the Spirit.[103] In the Old Testament stories of offerings, Ambrose found Jesus and Holy Spirit, including baptism with the Spirit and fire, spoken of.[104] Similarly Gideon, the charismatic judge, yields lessons about the Holy Spirit.[105]

Biblical teaching was also invoked when establishing the deity of the Spirit. At times, a slight biblical reference was seen as sufficient evidence of deity: such as to the "eternal" Spirit (Heb. 9:14),[106] or the fact that if in the Bible the Father and Son are called Spirit, then—by force of logic—it is obvious that the Spirit is divine as well![107] Another evidence of the Spirit's deity was found in the biblical statement that Christ (whose deity had been firmly established by this time) lives in us through the Spirit of God, which implies the similarity of nature among all three Trinitarian members.[108] Similarly, the Great Commission's command to baptize in the name of the Father, Son, and Spirit leads to the conviction of the shared divine nature.[109]

Yet another way of affirming the deity is based on the Spirit's nature as incorporeal and immutable, which follow from his salvific work among corporeal and changing human beings, implying that the Spirit, similarly to the Father and Son, is divine.[110] The same kind of method is followed in Ambrose's reasoning that the forgiveness of sins is an evidence of the Spirit's deity since it is a task also performed by Father and Son.[111] The conclusion reached by Hilary is thus inevitable: "When we hear the name *Father*, is not sonship involved in that Name? The Holy Ghost is mentioned by name; must He not exist? We can no more separate fatherhood from the Father or sonship from the Son than we can deny the existence in the Holy Ghost of that gift which we receive."[112]

While the greatest Latin father, St. Augustine, knows a number of names for the third person of the Trinity, three stand out in his theology, namely, Holy Spirit, Spirit as Love, and Spirit as Gift. All these he found in the biblical teaching. The bishop of Hippo reminds us of the fact that while both Father and Son are called "holy" and "spirit" in the Bible—indeed, "the Trinity can be called also the Holy Spirit"—what makes the third person unique is that the "Holy Spirit is a certain unutterable communion of the Father and the Son."[113] In other words, "He is the Spirit of the Father and Son, as the substantial and consubstantial love of both."[114] This reasoning also refers to the nature of the Spirit as the bond of love, a favorite designation of Augustine. Again, while acknowledging the fact that any of the members of the Trinity could be called Love, on the basis of biblical passages such as 1 John 4:7–19 and Romans 5:5, he comes to the conclusion that the Spirit particularly can be called Love, the bond of love uniting Father and Son, and derivatively, uniting the triune God and human beings.[115] The third biblical designation dear to Augustine is "gift." Passages such as Acts 2:38 specifically name the Spirit as "gift,"[116] while other New Testament allusions, such as John 7:37[117] and particularly Romans 5:5,[118] refer to the reception in the human heart of the Spirit.

The New Testament statements such as "God is Spirit" (John 4:24) and "For the Lord is Spirit, and where the Spirit of the Lord is, there is liberty" (2 Cor. 3:17) helped clarify the twofold reference of the term Spirit: on the one hand, it speaks of God's nature as "invisible and incomprehensible," and on the other hand, as the Gift of God given to the believer—in other words, as the name of the third person of the Trinity.[119]

The Consolidation of the Doctrine of the Spirit

While the Eastern fathers, as explained above, did not dare to call the Spirit God even when they fully affirmed the Spirit's divinity, Augustine does so, by calling the Holy Spirit "Very God, Equal with the Father and the Son."[120]

The following statements from the bishop of Hippo come as close as any in formulating the official opinion of the Western church. They invoke the teaching of both the Bible and tradition and set forth the doctrine of the Spirit in the framework of the Trinity:

> All those Catholic expounders of the divine Scriptures, both Old and New, whom I have been able to read, who have written before me concerning the Trinity, Who is God, have purposed to teach, according to the Scriptures, this doctrine, that the Father, and the Son, and the Holy Spirit intimate a divine unity of one and the same substance in an indivisible equality; and therefore that they are not three Gods, but one God: although the Father hath begotten the Son, and so He who is the Father is not the Son; and the Son is begotten by the Father, and so He who is the Son is not the Father; and the Holy Spirit is neither the Father nor the Son, but only the Spirit of the Father and of the Son, Himself also co-equal with the Father and the Son, and pertaining to the unity of the Trinity.[121]

> Therefore let us with steadfast piety believe in one God, the Father, and the Son, and the Holy Spirit; let us at the same time believe that the Son is not [the person] who is the Father, and the Father is not [the person] who is the Son, and neither the Father nor the Son is [the person] who is the Spirit of both the Father and the Son. Let it not be supposed that in this Trinity there is any separation in respect of time or place, but that these Three are equal and co-eternal, and absolutely of one nature: and that the creatures have been made, not some by the Father, and some by the Son, and some

by the Holy Spirit, but that each and all that have been or are now being created subsist in the Trinity as their Creator; and that no one is saved by the Father without the Son and the Holy Spirit, or by the Son without the Father and the Holy Spirit, or by the Holy Spirit without the Father and the Son, but by the Father, the Son, and the Holy Spirit, the only one, true, and truly immortal (that is, absolutely unchangeable) God.[122]

Trinitarian pneumatology lends itself naturally to affirming the mutual relationship of the Spirit and Christ. This mutual conditioning came to the fore already in the annunciation and conception of Jesus in the Virgin Mary.[123] The mutuality is also manifested in that the Spirit is not only sent by Jesus but that Jesus, similarly, was sent by the Spirit:

> The Spirit was upon Christ; and . . . as He sent the Spirit, so the Spirit sent the Son of God. For the Son of God says: "The Spirit of the Lord is upon Me, because He hath anointed Me, He hath sent Me to preach the Gospel to the poor, to proclaim liberty to the captives, and sight to the blind."[124]

No wonder, then, that the Spirit and Son also share mutual tasks, such as the work of judgment and punishment.[125]

The Holy Spirit as Uncreated Grace

Similarly to their Greek-speaking counterparts, the Latin-speaking fathers highlighted the *perichoretic* ("mutual indwelling") relationship among the Trinitarian members. An important corollary to this was the connecting of the inner-Trinitarian *perichoresis* with the economy of salvation in relation to the Spirit's work in the hearts of the human person:

> For as the Father is in the Son, and the Son in the Father, so, too, "the love of God is shed abroad in our hearts by the Holy Spirit, Who hath been given us." And as he who is blessed in Christ is blessed in the Name of the Father, and of the Son, and of the Holy Spirit, because the Name is one and the Power one; so, too, when any divine operation, whether of the Father, or of the Son, or of the Holy Spirit, is treated of, it is not referred only to the Holy Spirit, but also to the Father and the Son, and not only to the Father, but also to the Son and the Spirit.[126]

This important theological statement leads us to consider the role of the Spirit with regard to salvation, a key topic for both Eastern and Latin fathers yet developed in somewhat different ways. While the soteriology of the Christian West is often—rightly!—blamed by Eastern theologians for a lack of pneumatological orientation, this is not to say that for theologians such as St. Augustine, the Spirit does not play an important role in salvation and that soteriology is only a function of Christology. Indeed, for Augustine the Holy Spirit is the uncreated grace (*gratia increata*) given to humans. Thus, grace and justification are understood as the actual effect of the Holy Spirit.

The first passage from chapter 5 in *The Spirit and Letter*—in which the bishop most clearly presents his mature theology of salvation in pneumatological terms—titled "True Grace is the Gift of the Holy Ghost, Which Kindles in the Soul the Joy and Love of Goodness," teaches that the human person aided by the grace that comes from the Holy Spirit is able to advance in the Christian life; only when the human person receives the Holy Spirit is he divinely assisted in forming "in his mind a delight in, and a love of, that supreme and unchangeable good which is God."[127] This is to reverse the main effect of the fall, which for the bishop is perverted love: instead of loving God, the human person turns to anything created. The reception of the Holy Spirit as gift (or grace) makes it possible for the human person to fulfill the commandments of the law.[128] Augustine surmised that this grace was hidden in the Old Testament economy but made known and available through the Spirit for the New Testament economy of salvation.[129]

The Growing Institutionalization of the Economy of the Spirit

While charismatic manifestations did not end even when the Christian canon was finally ratified in the latter part of the fourth century—think of the teaching about the diversities of spiritual gifts and ministries by Hilary implying that those kinds of gifts were operative in the church[130]—with the consolidation of the "official" doctrine of the Spirit came also a strengthening of the "ecclesial control" over the Spirit's salvific work. In Augustine's theology in general and pneumatology in particular, the church plays a critical role. Augustine taught that the Holy Spirit can only be received in the church; this tendency was intensified especially in the conflict with the Donatist movement. Against his opponents, Augustine referred to and affirmed the opinion of the church that "the Holy Spirit is given by the imposition of hands in the Catholic Church only. . . ." Appeal to charismatic gifts of prophecy and the like—which Augustine acknowledged had been the case "in former days"—could not be seen as valid authorization alone anymore; rather, the claim to the Spirit by virtue of the laying on of hands by outsiders to the church was rather a statement against the unity of the church.[131]

Consequently, forgiveness is available only in the church;[132] forgiveness, while the act of the Holy Trinity, is specifically the work of the Holy Spirit.[133] Referring to Cyprian, whom we owe the ancient rule *extra ecclesiam nulla salus* ("outside the church there is no salvation"), Augustine thus concludes that those who separate themselves from the church, by that act are also separated from grace and Holy Spirit:

> He [Cyprian] says "that the Church, and the Spirit, and baptism, are mutually incapable of separation from each other, and therefore" he wishes that "those who are separated from the Church and the Holy Spirit should be understood to be separated also from baptism." But if this is the case, then when any one has received baptism in the Catholic Church, it remains so long in him as he himself remains in the Church, which is not so. For it is not restored to him when he returns, just because he did not lose it when he seceded. But as the disaffected sons have not the Holy Spirit in the same manner as the beloved sons, and yet they have baptism; so heretics also

have not the Church as Catholics have, and yet they have baptism. "For the Holy Spirit of discipline will flee deceit," and yet baptism will not flee from it. And so, as baptism can continue in one from whom the Holy Spirit withdraws Himself, so can baptism continue where the Church is not. But if "the laying on of hands" were not "applied to one coming from heresy," he would be as it were judged to be wholly blameless; but for the uniting of love, which is the greatest gift of the Holy Spirit, without which any other holy thing that there may be in a man is profitless to his salvation, hands are laid on heretics when they are brought to a knowledge of the truth.[134]

The Holy Spirit in Creedal Statements

The clarification of the status and role of the Spirit in the Trinity and the Spirit's elevation to the same status as the Son (even when the two still tended to be regarded in some way or another as "inferior" to the Father as the source) took place gradually and through much theological and spiritual reflection. Indicative of the development of pneumatological canons is the simple fact that whereas at the Council of Nicea in 325, the statement on the third person of the Trinity is very short, "And [we believe] in the Holy Ghost,"[135] in the Creed of Constantinople I (381)[136] the consubstantiality of the Spirit was officially confirmed: "And [we believe] in the Holy Ghost, the Lord and Giver-of-Life, who proceedeth from the Father, who with the Father and the Son together is worshipped and glorified, who spake by the prophets."[137]

A number of important affirmations about the Holy Spirit in the Nicene-Constantinopolitan Creed call for highlighting. First, the equal status of the Spirit was officially confirmed in that the Holy Spirit is to be "worshiped and glorified together with the Father and the Son."[138] Related to this is the mention of the proceeding of the Spirit from the Father, reminding us of the Trinitarian structure of the creed and confession of faith in the Spirit; here I am following the original text of the creed rather than the early amended text that also makes the derivation of the Spirit from the Son (this so-called filioque question will be dealt with in the medieval section).

Second, naming the Spirit the "Giver-of-Life" makes an integral connection with the doctrine of salvation. Now, it may be the case that this expression also relates to the key biblical teaching about the Spirit as the principle of life in general. It is safe to assume, however, that the soteriological function was really in the forefront. Historical developments confirm this: from early on, the main locus for the discussion of the Spirit both in Eastern and Western theology became soteriology, the doctrine of salvation, particularly the "subjective" reception of the benefits of Christ's "objective" work of redemption at the cross and resurrection. Third, the soteriological connection is brought home also in the nomenclature *Holy* Ghost, in other words, the Spirit's sanctifying work in the life of the believers.

Fourth, in keeping with later theological developments, the connection between the inspiration of prophetic Scripture and the Holy Spirit was established at

Constantinople. This statement follows the New Testament understanding of Scripture (first the Old Testament, then derivatively the New Testament) as "breathed-in" by the Holy Spirit (2 Tim. 3:16), echoing the "breathing-in" of Yahweh's Spirit in the nostrils of the first human being (Gen. 2:7). Not coincidentally, the New Testament at times also seems to call all of Scripture a "prophetic" word, which was believed to be made such by the Holy Spirit (2 Pet. 1:20–21, among others).

Fifth, considering more widely the whole context of the third article of the creed, in which the pneumatological statement is located, calls for two important remarks. It mentions the ecclesiological, particularly the liturgical, context for the confession of faith in the Holy Spirit: the Spirit will be lifted up and celebrated at the church's worship. The ecclesiological connection is further enhanced by the statement about belief in the one, holy, apostolic, and catholic church and the communion of saints immediately following belief in the Spirit. It might also be significant in this regard that this same article mentions, after the Spirit and the church, belief in the forgiveness of sins. Soteriological and ecclesiological themes are interrelated in that according to the earliest faith of Christians, salvation and forgiveness can only be had in the church. Furthermore, there is not only the ecclesiological but also the eschatological context for the confession of the Spirit. The article ends with a statement about the resurrection of the body and eternal life. While later theology by and large missed the integral connection between eschatology and pneumatology, in the biblical testimonies—as noted above—the link is established with the expectation and fulfillment of the pouring out of the Spirit as the launching of the final days (Joel 2 and Acts 2).

Chapter 3

Experiences of the Spirit in Medieval Theologies and Spiritualities

In any investigation of the almost millennium-long tradition of medieval pneumatologies, two overarching guidelines should be kept in mind.[1] First, by and large, theologians of this time period built on the patristic orientations, and only in few cases did they bring about distinctively novel inventions. In other words, in the aftermath of the careful theological reflection of the Fathers that culminated in creedal formulations, the main outline of pneumatological doctrine was considered to be in place. One theologically and ecumenically critical development in pneumatology belongs to this time period, namely, the so-called filioque debate, which has to do with the derivation of the Spirit in the Trinity—yet even its roots go back to the time of Augustine and other Latin fathers. The meaning and implications of that creedal addition will be reflected on in what follows. Second, even more than in the patristic period, medieval theology and spirituality of the Spirit show intensifying diversity and plurality. While mystical visions and experiences of the Spirit were not missing in earlier times, during the medieval period both in the Christian East and West, rich and variegated traditions of mysticism emerge.

In order to get a handle on such a diverse mass of testimonies and experiences of the Spirit, after a brief consideration of the question of the filioque, this discussion is divided into three parts. The first group of pneumatological traditions comes from what after the split of the Christian Church in 1054 came to be known as the Christian East.[2] Following the Eastern Christian testimonies, the experiences and testimonies of the rich and variegated mystical spirituality of the (High) Middle Ages represented by saints such as Hildegard of Bingen and Bernard of Clairvaux will be presented. Third, the "scholastic" or "mainstream" pneumatologies of the Christian West led by the Angelic Doctor Thomas Aquinas will be discussed.

THE FILIOQUE QUESTION AND THE SPLIT BETWEEN THE CHRISTIAN EAST AND WEST

The term *filioque* (Latin: "and from the Son") refers to the addition by Latin Christianity to the Niceno-Constantinopolitan Creed of 381 concerning the dual procession of the Spirit both from the Son and the Father. The original form of the creed said that the Holy Spirit "proceeds from the Father." While some of the historical details are debated,[3] it is clear that in the first major breach of the Christian church in 1054 the filioque clause played a major role along with political, ecclesiastical, and cultural issues.

The reasons for the insertion of the dual procession into the creed are both biblical and historical. The New Testament is ambiguous about the procession of the Spirit. On the one hand, the Johannine Jesus says that he himself will send the Spirit (John 16:7) or that he will send the Spirit (called *Parakletos* here) who proceeds from the Father (15:26). On the other hand, Jesus prays to the Father to send the Spirit (14:16) and says the Father will send the Spirit in Jesus' name (14:26). Furthermore, the Augustinian idea of the Spirit as shared love, followed by that of other Latin writers, contributed to the rise of the idea of the procession of the Spirit from both the Father and Son. Scholars wonder if the addition also served a function in opposing Arianism. Mentioning the Son alongside the Father as the origin of the Spirit was seen as a way to defend consubstantiality.[4]

From the beginning, the Christian East has objected vigorously to this addition, claiming that it was one-sided and added without ecumenical consultation,[5] that it compromises the monarchy of the Father as the source of divinity,[6] and that it subordinates the Spirit to Jesus with theological corollaries in ecclesiology, the doctrine of salvation, and so on.[7] Even with its exaggerations, the Eastern critique of the filioque is important both ecumenically and theologically and should not be dismissed.[8] The West did not have the right to unilaterally add filioque. At the same time, it can be argued that filioque is not heretical even though ecumenically and theologically it is unacceptable and therefore should be removed. This is the growing consensus of both Protestant and Roman Catholic theologians.[9] An alternative to filioque that reads "from the Father through the Son" would also be acceptable to the Christian East.[10] At the same time, it would be important for the East to be able to acknowledge the nonheretical nature of the addition.

THE SPIRIT IN MEDIEVAL
EASTERN CHRISTIAN TRADITIONS

The Spirit in a Trinitarian Cosmic Vision

A defining difference in orientation and method between the theological visions of the Christian East and West is the distinction between apophatic and kataphatic theologies. The apophatic orientation, typical of the East, is reluctant to offer clearly defined, "positive" (kataphatic) descriptions of divine mysteries (like those in Western theology) and instead approaches the mystical divine realities and symbols through "negative," indirect, suggestive terms. Spiritual vision and discernment is as important—or even more so—than intellectual acumen and shrewdness. The Holy Spirit is the key to such vision because "the things that are sealed up and closed, unseen and unknown by all men, are opened up by the Holy Spirit alone."[11] The use of symbols, metaphors, and poetic expressions fits in well with this kind of mystical orientation. Some of the most imaginative metaphors used for the Spirit in this tradition are the lamp and the key of the door![12]

In Eastern Christianity, the Trinity is present everywhere. In pneumatology this Trinitarian orientation also comes to the fore in a most profound Spirit-Christology. Through Christ's incarnation human beings are introduced to the Father, and through the Spirit's work they are reconciled to God. The incarnation itself is a highly Trinitarian and pneumatological event:

> In becoming incarnate, the Word of God teaches us the mystical knowledge of God because he shows us in himself the Father and the Holy Spirit. For the full Father and the full Holy Spirit are essentially and completely in the full Son, even the incarnate Son, without being themselves incarnate. Rather, the Father gives approval and the Spirit cooperates in the incarnation with the Son who . . . gives adoption by giving through the Spirit a supernatural birth from on high in grace.[13]

Indicative of the thick mystical underpinnings of Eastern Orthodox spiritualities is *Mystical Theology* and the rest of the body of writings of the fifth- or sixth-century pseudonymous mystic Dionysius the Areopagite—perhaps a Syrian monk with Platonic leanings.[14] Notwithstanding our lack of historical and biographical knowledge, the writings attributed to the Areopagite have exercised a profound influence both in the Christian East and West. In *The Divine Names*, Pseudo-Dionysius introduces a pneumatologically based apophatic theological vision:

> And here also let us set before our minds the scriptural rule that in speaking about God we should declare the Truth, not with enticing words of man's wisdom, but in demonstration of the power which the Spirit stirred up in the Sacred Writers, whereby, in a manner surpassing speech and knowledge, we embrace those truths which, in like manner, surpass them, in that Union which exceeds our faculty, and exercise of discursive, and

of intuitive reason. We must not then dare to speak, or indeed to form any conception, of the hidden super-essential Godhead, except those things that are revealed to us from the Holy Scriptures.[15]

Among Eastern theologians who joined in the spiritual apophatic vision of the Areopagite, few are more remarkable than the seventh-century theologian and monk Saint Maximus the Confessor,[16] whose influence similarly is also felt in the Christian West. In keeping with the apophatic theological method and the all-important soteriological vision of *theosis*—that is, deification—prayer and purity of mind are considered prerequisites to a "spiritual contemplation" and seeing the "invisible things" of divine mysteries.[17] In the divine liturgy "the soul . . . comes as into a church to an inviolable shelter of peace in the natural contemplation in the Spirit" and "by the prayer through which we are made worthy to call God our Father we receive the truest adoption in the grace of the Holy Spirit."[18]

Not only mystical and apophatic, Eastern theology in general and pneumatology—as well as ecclesiology—in particular are more communal and cosmic in orientation. This correlates with the idea of the human person having been created in the image of God as the "minicosmos" and of the church patterned in the image of the triune God—similarly the whole cosmos in miniature. The work of the Spirit, consequently, is often perceived in universal, cosmic terms.

In one of the most unique—even astonishing—statements about the Holy Spirit, Maximus names the Spirit as the kingdom of God: "The kingdom of God the Father who subsists essentially is the Holy Spirit. Indeed, what Matthew here [in The Lord's Prayer] calls kingdom another evangelist elsewhere calls Holy Spirit: 'May your Holy Spirit come and purify us.'"[19] This insight is related to the cosmic presence of the Spirit in the created order, particularly in all intelligent beings. What is remarkable about this teaching is that it links together the Spirit's presence in nature as the principle of life; the Spirit's work as the basis for distinctively human life, including intelligence and morality; and the Spirit's deifying work.

The Holy Spirit is not absent from any created being, especially not from one that in any way participates in intelligence. For being God and God's Spirit, he embraces in unity the spiritual knowledge of all created things, providentially permeating all things with his power and vivifying their inner essences in accordance with their nature. In this way he makes people aware of things done sinfully against the law of nature and renders them capable of choosing principles that are true and in conformity with nature. Thus we find many barbarians and nomadic peoples turning to a civilized way of life and setting aside the savage laws that they had kept among themselves from time immemorial.

> The Holy Spirit is present unconditionally in all things, in that He embraces all things, provides for all, and vivifies the natural seeds within them. He is present in a specific way in all who are under the Law, in that He shows them where they have broken the commandments and enlightens them

about the promise given concerning Christ. In all who are Christians He is present also in yet another way in that He makes them sons of God. But in none is He fully present as the author of wisdom except in those who have understanding, and who by their holy way of life have made themselves fit to receive His indwelling and deifying presence.[20]

Deification as the Goal of Salvation

Medieval Eastern theology followed in the footsteps of the Fathers in affirming everywhere the vision of salvation as true participation in God. While true participation, the charge of pantheism is avoided by the distinction between God's essence and energies: deification means partaking in the very energies of the Spirit even though the finite human being can never be part of God's essence. Consequently, the nomenclature "deifying" appears frequently in talk about the Holy Spirit.[21] Symeon the New Theologian explains the meaning of deification under the heading "God as the Light of the Soul":

> Man is united to God spiritually and physically, since the soul is not separated from the mind, neither the body from the soul. By being united in essence man also has three hypostases by grace. He is a single god by adoption with body and soul and the divine Spirit, of whom he has become a partaker. Then is fulfilled what was spoken by the prophet David, "I have said, ye are gods, and ye are all the sons of the Most High" (Ps. 82:6), that is, sons of the Most High according to the image of the Most High and according to His likeness (Gen. 1:26). We become the divine offspring of the Divine Spirit (Jn.3:8), to whom the Lord rightly said and continues to say, "Abide in Me, that you may bring forth much fruit" (Jn. 15:4, 8). . . . It is evident that just as the Father abides in His own Son (Jn. 14:10) and the Son in His Father's bosom (Jn. 1:18) by nature, so those who have been born anew through the divine Spirit (Jn. 3:3, 5) and by His gift have become the brothers of Christ our God and sons of God and gods by adoption, by grace abide in God and God in them (1 John 4:12ff.).[22]

No other postpatristic Father has expounded so powerfully and convincingly the meaning and implications of the distinctive Christian East's vision of salvation as *theosis* or deification than Gregory of Palamas. In his theology, one can easily discern the underlying theological anthropology of the East in which the human being as *image of God* is believed to be able to receive the deifying grace of the Holy Spirit: "So, when the saints contemplate this divine light within themselves, seeing it by the divinising communion of the Spirit, through the mysterious visitation of perfecting illuminations—then they behold the garment of their deification, their mind being glorified and filled by the grace of the Word, beautiful beyond measure in His splendour."[23]

As mentioned before, it is in the divine liturgy and sacraments—usually named "mysteries" in the Eastern tradition—that the work of the Spirit in deification takes place most profoundly. In holy baptism, "our soul, purified by the Spirit, becomes brighter than the sun," making it possible to see the glory of God.[24]

Often deification is described in terms of "seeing the light," which is spiritual seeing beyond just the knowledge of God.[25] So intense is the belief in deification that at times the deified human person already in this age can be named "light and spirit"![26]

The Pursuit of True Spirituality

In addition to a more positive anthropology, Eastern spirituality also emphasizes asceticism, prayers, and other spiritual exercises as a way to a deeper spirituality. These are not considered to be merits (indeed, in the Christian East, the Augustinian-Pelagian debates are totally unknown) but rather proper and necessary responses to the grace of God. Pursuing the ways of the Spirit and the will of God also leads to the acquiring of charisms.

Symeon the New Theologian's spiritual manual *The Discourses* offers profound insights into and lessons about acquiring and maintaining the Spirit. Not revealing the name of "our holy father," Symeon lists the proper qualities of a saint who not only overflows with the life of the Spirit but is also able to communicate it to others:

> Just as a cistern is filled by running water, so our holy father partook of the fullness of our Master Jesus Christ and was filled by the grace of His Spirit, which is "living water" (Jn. 4:10). A man may take water from a cistern that overflows and runs down on the outside till his thirst is quenched. Similarly we have seen and have received from our holy father that which overflowed and constantly poured over; we drank of it and washed our faces with it, even our hands and feet, and bathed our entire bodies (Jn. 13:9f) and our very souls with that immortal water."[27]

True spirituality can also be briefly defined as the combination of orthodox faith, "praiseworthy life," and the gift of the Spirit and the Spirit's gifts. This results in the praise of the whole church.[28] Prayer, ascetic exercises, and at times even "tears"[29] are recommended as means of enhancing the reception of the Spirit. Consequently, unlike Protestant traditions, which are reserved about making distinctions between various levels of sanctification, in the Christian East such distinctions are typical because of the stress on divine-human *synergia*. St. Gregory of Sinai, well known for his ceaseless prayer life, surmised that if "our nature is not kept immaculate by the Spirit, or is not purified as it should be, then body and soul cannot be one with Christ, now and in the future resurrection." To maintain deification and sanctification, Christians are in need of constant "renewal by the Spirit." Because there are varying levels of dedication, Gregory opined—in analogy with many mansions Jesus spoke of—there will be "different degrees of existence in the other world" according to one's level of purification. He also refers to Paul's teaching about various levels of lights in the analogy of shining stars. Even more boldly, this spiritual director maintains that even in the life to come the saints, along with angels, keep on progressing in "increasing their gifts . . . [and] striving for greater and ever greater blessings."[30]

With this lofty goal in mind, Gregory didn't have much patience for those preachers and teachers in the church who spoke of the Spirit but didn't obviously have the Spirit working actively in their own lives.[31]

No wonder that the mystical spirituality of the Eastern Church holds the charismatic energies of the Spirit in high regard. In keeping with the synergetic orientation of spirituality, the manifestations of the Spirit are considered to be given according to the measure of the Christian's faith and dedication.[32]

MYSTICAL EXPERIENCES OF THE SPIRIT IN THE WEST

Veni Spiritus Creator

A fitting way to introduce the medieval mystical experiences of the Spirit in the West is to listen to the perhaps most-famous hymn ever written to the Spirit, known as "*Veni Spiritus Creator*" ("Come, Creator Spirit").[33] Although scholarly consensus is lacking, an old tradition attributes the hymn to Gregory the Great, often called the "last Latin father," the sixth-century pope and great advocate of the office of the primacy.

> Creator-Spirit, all-Divine,
> Come, visit every soul of Thine,
> And fill with Thy celestial flame
> The hearts which Thou Thyself didst frame.
> O gift of God, Thine is the sweet
> Consoling name of Paraclete—
> And spring of life and fire and love
> And unction flowing from above.
> The mystic sevenfold gifts are Thine,
> Finger of God's right hand divine;
> The Father's promise sent to teach
> The tongue a rich and heavenly speech.
> Kindle with fire brought from above
> Each sense, and fill our hearts with love;
> And grant our flesh, so weak and frail,
> The strength of Thine which cannot fail.
> Drive far away our deadly foe.
> And grant us Thy true peace to know;
> So we, led by Thy guidance still,
> May safely pass through every ill.
> To us, through Thee, the grace be shown
> To know the Father and the Son;
> And Spirit of Them both, may we
> Forever rest our faith in Thee.
> To Sire and Son be praises meet,
> And to the Holy Paraclete;
> And may Christ send us from above
> That Holy Spirit's gift of love.

Authorization and Empowerment by the Holy Spirit

The medieval mystics experienced the ministry of the Holy Spirit in several different ways, from gifting to divine authorization to miracles to extraordinary experiences. Similarly to their Eastern counterparts, these Western mystics regarded spiritual experience very highly and saw in it an excellent gateway into spiritual wisdom. Best known for his multivolume commentary *On the Song of Songs*, the twelfth-century Bernard of Clairvaux was passionate about reviving both monastic (especially Cistercian) and popular spirituality. Not unlike some other mystics, Bernard was at times doctrinally suspect and socially as well as emotionally troubled. Reflecting on the saying in the *Song of Songs* concerning the kiss between the bride and bridegroom—which is related to the Holy Spirit, as we will see below— Bernard turns to spiritual experience as the highest way of knowledge:

> Today the text we are to study is the book of our own experience. You must therefore turn your attention inwards, each one must take note of his own particular awareness of the things I am about to discuss. . . . Any one who has received this mystical kiss from the mouth of Christ at least once, seeks again that intimate experience, and eagerly looks for its frequent renewal. I think that nobody can grasp what it is except the one who receives it.[34]

The year 1998 was the nine hundredth birthday of Bernard's contemporary, the Benedictine Hildegard of Bingen. This multitalented woman was a theologian, herbalist, composer, visionary, and a prophet. In her theological magnum opus *Scivias*, she claims a profound spiritual authority by virtue of the power of the Holy Spirit:

> "O you who are wretched earth, and, as a woman, untaught in all learning of earthly teachers and unable to read literature with philosophical understanding, you are nonetheless touched by My light, which kindles in you an inner fire like a burning sun; cry out and relate and write these My mysteries that you see and hear in mystical visions. So do not be timid, but say those things you understand in the Spirit as I speak them through you."[35]

In a profound way, Hildegard testifies to having been addressed by the Almighty who had commissioned her to spread the true knowledge and spirituality:

> And behold, He Who was enthroned upon that mountain cried out in a strong, loud voice saying, "O human, who are fragile dust of the earth and ashes of ashes! Cry out and speak of the origin of pure salvation until those people are instructed, who, though they see the inmost contents of the Scriptures, do not wish to tell them or preach them, because they are lukewarm and sluggish in serving God's justice. Unlock for them the enclosure of mysteries that they, timid as they are, conceal in a hidden and fruitless field. Burst forth into a fountain of abundance and overflow with mystical knowledge. . . . For you have received your profound insight not from humans, but from the lofty and tremendous Judge on high, where this calmness will shine strongly with glorious light among the shining ones."[36]

The acknowledgment of this kind of spiritual authority is extraordinary in the life of a woman in any time period, particularly at Hildegard's time. She was not the only one who felt she had received spiritual authority and commissioning through the Spirit. The most well-known Scandinavian mystic, the fourteenth-century Birgitta (or Bridget) of Sweden, who received her first vision at the age of seven, similarly claimed divine authorization.[37] *The Life of Blessed Birgitta* records that the Lady from Sweden had the gift of the prophetic word: secrets of the heart were revealed to her through the Spirit. Furthermore, Birgitta received *Heavenly Revelations* in the form of a book, as well as "in the *Book of Questions,* which was also given to her divinely, through an infusion from the Holy Spirit, in a wonderful manner and, as it were, in a single hour." Visual experiences were also given to her.[38] Julian of Norwich's *Revelations of Divine Love* similarly testify to the reception of insight into the Trinity via the experience of the Spirit.[39] Birgitta's contemporary Catherine of Siena claims to have received her first vision as young as the age of six. Her contemporaries believed she had the gift of healing. Tradition even attributes to her a "mystical death" at the end of her life of service and dedication to all the needy.

A profoundly eschatological-apocalyptic turn of mysticism was represented by perhaps the most significant prophet of the Middle Ages in the Christian West, Joachim of Fiore. He was a man of visions and spiritual experiences par excellence. The Abbot of a Cistercian monastery, Joachim divided history in three periods, those of the Father, of the Son, and finally of the Spirit, the end-time apocalyptic pouring out of the Spirit ushering in the end. The last era, that of the Spirit, started off with St. Benedictine, whom Joachim admired greatly. Fond of typologies and cycles, Joachim spoke of the highest order of the "elect," namely the monastic order, above the orders of the married and the clergy, and attributes its excellency to the Holy Spirit.[40] As with many mystics, for Joachim the "revelatory" insights from the Holy Spirit for helping understand divine mysteries, such as the Trinity, were not uncommon at all.[41]

Metaphors of the Spirit

Catherine's female sensitivities come to expression in the way she speaks of the tender care of the Holy Spirit in terms of motherly love: "Such a soul has the Holy Spirit as a mother who nurses her at the breast of divine charity. The Holy Spirit has set her free, releasing her, as her lord, from the slavery of selfish love. . . . This servant, the Holy Spirit, whom I in my providence have given her, clothes her, nurtures her, inebriates her with tenderness and the greatest wealth."[42] In some of the most striking passages, she speaks of the Holy Spirit as the waitress at the celebration of the Eucharist along with the Father, who is the "table," and the Son, "our food." In this "table of the Lamb," the Spirit-waitress is constantly "serving us every grace and gift, spiritual as well as material."[43]

A faithful Catholic looking at Mary the Mother God, Catherine saw "the Holy Spirit's hand . . . the Trinity [having been written] in you by forming within you the incarnate Word, God's only-begotten Son."[44] Catherine's metaphors also include the striking images of the Holy Spirit as "servant" and "laborer, the most merciful free-flowing Holy Spirit . . . the strong hand that held the Word nailed fast to the cross"![45]

To Bernard of Clairvaux, we owe several striking metaphors used of the Holy Spirit. Imagining the Spirit as the Kiss of the Father and Son as well as that between the Bride and the church is one of the most intriguing ones in Christian literature:

> The bride, although otherwise so audacious, does not dare to say: "Let him kiss me with his mouth," for she knows that this is the prerogative of the Father alone. What she does ask for is something less: "Let him kiss me with the kiss of his mouth." Do you wish to see the newly-chosen bride receiving this unprecedented kiss, given not by the mouth but by the kiss of the mouth? Then look at Jesus in the presence of his Apostles: "He breathed on them," according to St John, "and he said: 'Receive the Holy Spirit.'" That favor, given to the newly-chosen Church, was indeed a kiss. That? you say. That corporeal breathing? O no, but rather the invisible Spirit, who is so bestowed in that breath of the Lord that he is understood to proceed from him equally as from the Father, truly the kiss that is common both to him who kisses and to him who is kissed. Hence the bride is satisfied to receive the kiss of the Bridegroom, though she be not kissed with his mouth. For her it is no mean or contemptible thing to be kissed by the kiss, because it is nothing less than the gift of the Holy Spirit.[46]

Salvation as Union

While the favorite Eastern term *theosis* is only rarely used, the idea of union between the human being and God is common in many spiritualities and theologies of the Christian West as well. The thirteenth-century Johannes Eckhart, known as Meister Eckhart (from the German academic title "Master"), explained this union in a way that is not only thoroughly mystical but also betrays typical Eastern features. Brushing aside the primacy of intelligence and will—typical "scholastic" theologians' way of understanding grace—this leading mystic thinks of grace in terms of the divine "spark":

> Grace never comes in the intelligence or in the will. If it could come in the intelligence or in the will, the intelligence and the will would have to transcend themselves. On this a master says: There is something secret about it; and thereby he means the spark of the soul, which alone can apprehend God. The true union between God and the soul takes place in the little spark, which is called the spirit of the soul. Grace unites not to any work. It is an indwelling and a living together of the soul in God.[47]

Again, similarly to Eastern traditions, purification and sanctification are seen as the highest form of union; these help elevate the human person into a stage that "he may most resemble the ideal of himself which existed in God, before God created men."[48] This vision of progressing in sanctification and charity is very much part of Bernard's teaching in his spiritual manual *The Steps of Humility and Praise.*[49]

"SCHOLASTIC" TEACHING ABOUT PNEUMATOLOGY

The Holy Spirit and Grace

Whereas the mystics of the West focused on spiritual experiences, including various prophetic and other charismatic gifts, as well as cultivating both monastic and lay spirituality, the "schoolmen" devoted their best intellectual capacities to continuing doctrinal work. Some of them, such as the "Angelic Doctor" Thomas Aquinas, while no stranger to spiritual experiences either, made profound doctrinal contributions, whereas others, particularly Bonaventure—in his main work *The Soul's Journey to God*—cast the theological vision into the form of spirituality. Fittingly it has been said that "while Thomas Aquinas supplied the great medieval theological synthesis for Western Christianity, Bonaventure provided one of the most important spiritual syntheses."[50] Bonaventure's great interest in spirituality is also shown in his work with Francis of Assisi's biography.

One of the areas in which scholastic theology advanced the pneumatological doctrine inherited from the Fathers is the Spirit's ministry in salvation. Both Aquinas and Bonaventure left lasting marks on the doctrine of grace. While owing to Augustine, Thomas is also critical of the Bishop's identification of grace with the Spirit given to the heart of the believer. While for Augustine, God/Spirit is not only the giver but also the gift, that is, the personal presence of God in the heart of the believer, for Thomas grace and love spring from the Holy Spirit who then sets the soul in motion acquiring the justifying grace. Unlike Augustine's view (*On the Trinity*, 15.17), Thomas affirms that grace (charity) is created in the soul, it is a "habitual gift." Grace, thus

> may be taken in two ways; first, as a Divine help, whereby God moves us to will and to act; secondly, as a habitual gift divinely bestowed on us. Now in both these ways grace is fittingly divided into operating and cooperating. For the operation of an effect is not attributed to the thing moved but to the mover. Hence in that effect in which our mind is moved and does not move, but in which God is the sole mover, the operation is attributed to God, and it is with reference to this that we speak of "operating grace." But in that effect in which our mind both moves and is moved, the operation is not only attributed to God, but also to the soul; and it is with reference to this that we speak of "cooperating grace." . . . And thus if grace is taken for God's gratuitous motion whereby He moves us to meritorious good, it is fittingly divided into operating and cooperating grace. . . . And thus habitual grace, inasmuch as it heals and justifies the soul, or makes it pleasing to God, is called operating grace; but inasmuch as it is the principle of meritorious works, which spring from the free-will, it is called cooperating grace.[51]

Bonaventure, who happened to be student in Paris at the same time as Thomas Aquinas, devoted one long chapter in his *Breviloquium* to the discussion of grace and the Spirit. Following his famous contemporary—and having treated the incarnation, which "is the source and fountain of every gratuitous gift"—he explains the meaning of grace as gift:

> As to grace, as a gift divinely given, we must hold that it is in itself a gift because it is given by God and flows immediately from Him. The Holy Ghost is given with it and in it and for He is an uncreated, excellent, and perfect gift. . . . Nevertheless, grace is a gift by which the soul is perfected and becomes the bride of Christ, the daughter of the eternal Father, and the temple of the Holy Ghost. . . . Grace, therefore, is a gift which cleanses, enlightens and perfects the soul, brings it to life, reforms it and strengthens it, lifts it up, likens and joins it to God and thereby makes it acceptable to God. Hence a gift of this kind is rightfully called and ought to be named a *gratia gratum faciens*. . . .[52]

The reason this grace is called *gratia gratum faciens* ("grace making gracious") is because it makes the human person pleasing to God.[53] When it comes to the counterpart concept, *gratia gratis data* ("grace(s) freely given"), Bonaventure explains—following the fine distinctions in Catholic theology between general, special, and proper grace:

> It is called general to denote it as a divine aid freely and liberally imparted to a creature and as indifferent in regard to any act. Without this kind of aiding grace we are unable to do anything or to continue in existence. Grace is called special when it is divinely given as an aid so that he who has prepared himself for the reception of the gift of the Holy Ghost may attain the state of merit with it, and such is called *gratia gratis data*, and without it no one can adequately do what it is in his power to do, namely, prepare himself for salvation.[54]

The Nature and Procession of the Holy Spirit

Appointed the Archbishop of Canterbury at the age of sixty, the Italian-born Anselm, one of the most brilliant and analytic medieval minds, discusses in his *Monologion* the nature and workings of the Spirit in a way that seems to us highly scholastic. Here the Benedictine theologian attempts to establish the absolute existence of the Spirit vis-à-vis the mutability and changeability of others:

> This Spirit exists in an unqualified sense; compared to it created things do not exist. Therefore . . . this Spirit, which exists in such a marvellously unique and uniquely marvellous way of its own, in a certain sense alone exists—while by comparison to it other things, whatever they are seen to be, do not exist. For if we take a close look, only this Spirit will be seen to exist in an unqualified sense and completely and absolutely; and everything else will be seen almost not to exist and scarcely to exist. On account of its immutable eternity this Spirit can be said unqualifiedly to exist; it cannot

be said, in accordance with some alteration, to have existed or to be going to exist. Nor is it, through being changeable, anything which at some time it was not or will not be; nor does it fail to be something which it once was or will be. Rather, whatever it is it is once, at once, and without limitation. Since, I say, it is this kind of being, it is rightly said to exist in an unqualified sense and absolutely and completely.[55]

The topic of the derivation of the Holy Spirit and the Spirit's relation to Father and Son occupied the best scholastic minds. In keeping with tradition, St. Thomas explained that the term "Holy Spirit" can be taken either as the proper name of the third person of the Trinity (in which case it is "one word") or as a designation of something common to the Father, Son, and Spirit (in which case it is "two words").[56] Similarly, the term "Love" can be taken either "essentially" or "personally." In the latter sense, it is the proper name of the third member of the Trinity.[57] Thus one of the key designations for the Holy Spirit is Love.

Thomas and others also established the terminology with regard to two processions in God: "one by way of the intellect, which is the procession of the Word, and another by way of the will, which is the procession of Love." Technically the former is known as "procession," and the latter, with regard to the Spirit, as "spiration."[58]

It had become customary in Western church theology not only to affirm the filioque clause but also to defend it theologically. Aquinas surmised that in case the Spirit does not also derive from the Son, it means that the Spirit could not be personally distinguished from Him. In other words, the distinctions in the divine essence are relational rather than "absolute." Because it would be absurd to say that the Son is from the Father, Thomas establishes the personal distinction by virtue of "opposite relations" only with the statement that the Spirit is from the Son.[59]

Similarly Anselm finds compelling reasons for the defense of filioque. His reasoning is based on the naming of the Father as "the memory of the Supreme Spirit," the Son as the "understanding," and the Spirit as the "memory." Anselm opines that it is impossible for the Supreme Spirit to love itself unless it remembers and understands itself. Now, here is Anselm's indubitable conclusion based on this logic: "So, clearly, the Supreme Spirit's love proceeds from its remembering and understanding itself. But if the Father is referred to as the memory of the Supreme Spirit, and if the Son is referred to as the understanding of the Supreme Spirit, then it is obvious that the love of the Supreme Spirit proceeds equally from the Father and the Son."[60] In his study *The Procession of the Holy Spirit*, the Bishop of Canterbury acknowledges that even though the Eastern church vehemently rejects the filioque clause, he hopes with all his heart that the Greek theologians' minds would be changed as a result of the force of this logic. Anselm assumes that all theologians agree on the starting point, which simply says that both Son and Spirit exist from the Father, though differently (for which tradition, as mentioned above, uses different terms denoting the origin). Since no theologian upholds the view that the Son is begotten from the Spirit (which would make the Spirit the Father of the Son) rather than from the Father or that the Son proceeds from the Spirit (which would make him "the spirit of the Holy Spirit"), it "follows by irrefutable reasoning that the Holy Spirit exists from the Son, even as He also exists from the Father."[61]

While the Christian East and West strongly disagree about the origin of the Holy Spirit in the Trinity, both traditions in their own distinctive ways affirm the mutual relationship between Jesus and the Spirit. The foundation of the Spirit-Christology was firmly established by the Fathers and further developed by the medieval theologians. In Bonaventure's main work *The Soul's Journey into God*, we find a profound Spirit-Christology. The conception of the Savior in the Blessed Virgin was brought about by the divine Spirit:

> Just as man was formed from the earth on the sixth day by the power and wisdom of the divine hand, so at the beginning of the sixth age, the Archangel Gabriel was sent to the Virgin. When she gave her consent to him, the Holy Spirit came upon her like a divine fire *in*flaming her soul and sanctifying her flesh in perfect purity.[62]

Subsequently, Jesus received the Spirit as he was baptized by John. Bonaventure calls the baptism of Jesus "the doorway of the sacraments and the foundation of virtues."[63] In his *Commentary on the Acts of the Apostles*, the eighth-century "Father of English History" Venerable Bede delves deeply into the sacramental and ecclesiological implications of Jesus' baptism. Bede sees a parallel between Jesus' anointing with the gift of grace at his baptism and the (ancient Christian) custom of anointing the baptismal candidates with oil.[64]

"Gratuitous Graces": Charisms

In response to his own question "Whether there is a gratuitous grace of working miracles?" the Angelic Doctor has an opportunity to explain the meaning of gifts:

> As stated above the Holy Ghost provides sufficiently for the Church in matters profitable unto salvation, to which purpose the gratuitous graces are directed. Now just as the knowledge which a man receives from God needs to be brought to the knowledge of others through the gift of tongues and the grace of the word, so too the word uttered needs to be confirmed in order that it be rendered credible. This is done by the working of miracles, according to Mk. 16:20, "And confirming the word with signs that followed": and reasonably so. For it is natural to man to arrive at the intelligible truth through its sensible effects. Wherefore just as man led by his natural reason is able to arrive at some knowledge of God through His natural effects, so is he brought to a certain degree of supernatural knowledge of the objects of faith by certain supernatural effects which are called miracles. Therefore the working of miracles belongs to a gratuitous grace.[65]

As always, Thomas presents a highly sophisticated analysis of any topic he takes up, in this case the issue of spiritual gifts. He distinguishes three aspects of "gratuitous graces": in relation to knowledge, speech, and operation. Prophecy is a case in point. Prophetic gifts have the knowledge element because prophetic revelation contains divinely granted knowledge of events otherwise unknown to human beings. Second, there is the speech element, for according to New Testament passages such as 1 Corinthians 12:7 and 14:12, the manifestations of the Spirit are meant for the upbuilding of the whole church; in order to serve as such, there must be sharing, declaration, and utterances from the prophets. Third, there is the operation element in that the goal of the prophetic revelation, including the discernment of the spirits, is to direct and correct behavior and acts.[66]

In his discussion of speaking in tongues, Thomas seems to support the idea of *xenolalia*, according to which tongues were given to the disciples for them to be able to proclaim the gospel in an understandable language (in contrast to unknown language, which is called *glossolalia*).[67] The Venerable Bede, in his exposition of the second chapter of the book of Acts, surmises that "the church's humility recovers the unity of languages which the pride of Babylon had shattered. Spiritually . . . the variety of languages signifies gifts of a variety of graces."[68]

Pentecost Hymn

While it is appropriate to make a distinction between the mystics and "scholastics" of the medieval era, that distinction can only be taken heuristically. As is well known, the Angelic Doctor Thomas had a powerful mystical experience toward the end of his life as a result of which his unsurpassed intellectual powers seemed to be of little value. Peter Abelard, the twelfth-century Parisian theologian and master of letters, penned a number of hymns, one of which is to be sung on the day of Pentecost.[69]

> The Holy Spirit comes to share
> His burning altar in our heart.
> Accept, O God, your temples there;
> With virtues dedicate their art.
> These are the sevenfold gifts you as God possess,
> Binding seven demons of wickedness.
> These your gifts are goodness and holiness.
>
> The *fear* of God can set us free,
> But wickedness must first abate.
> The poor on earth with such a key
> May enter rich in heaven's gate.
> You, Master, give us this; give to us graciously.
> Give the guilty less than the penalty.
> Yours the glory, yours be the victory.
>
> And give us force of *holiness*;
> Let not temptation overwhelm.

The mild and merciful possess
This grace and all the earthly realm.
And, Master, give us this.

Let *knowledge* fall on us as well,
Through which we know the grace of tears.
Your pardon casts its holy spell
When we have paid up all arrears.
And, Master, give us this.

With holy might your strength is shed
On those who thirst for righteousness.
The fulness of the very bread
Is vigor pilgrim souls express.
And, Master, give us this.

And give us highest *counsel*, Lord;
Hereto your mercy will suffice.
So may you then allow reward;
For this you ask, not sacrifice.
And, Master, give us this.

In *understanding* you are known
As God within the Trinity.
The pure in heart can see alone
The kingdom's high sublimity.
And, Master, give us this.

You give us *wisdom* finally,
In which the Sons of God take rest.
The name of father makes them free
To sanctify what there is blest.
And, Master, give us this.

By force of the apostles' prayers
Whom you renewed at Pentecost,
Give us the graces such as theirs,
And strengthen us lest we be lost.
These are the sevenfold gifts you as God possess,
Binding seven demons of wickedness.
These your gifts are goodness and holiness.

Chapter 4

The Holy Spirit
in Reformation Theologies

The statement on Reformation theologies of the Spirit by the Roman Catholic Yves Congar in his celebrated *I Believe in the Holy Spirit*, helps set the stage for this chapter's discussion:

> Luther and Calvin . . . kept to the classical teaching of Nicea and Constantinople (381) and even to the Creed *Quicumque*[1] with regard to the Trinity. Both had to fight on two fronts. On the one hand, they had to combat entrenched "Catholic" positions which were rightly or wrongly identified with a need to regard the "Church," or rather the "hierarchy," as absolute. On the other hand, they had to fight against "enthusiasts" who appealed to the Spirit in their claim that they were furthering the reforming movement. The enthusiasts whom Luther had to resist were the *Schwärmer*[2] Storch, Müntzer and Karlstadt, and those whom Calvin opposed were the Anabaptists. Both Reformers kept to a middle road, or rather a synthesis, and each in his own way insisted on a close relationship between an external "instrument" of grace—Scripture—and the activity of the Spirit.[3]

The three main theological and spiritual movements that form the Reformation period serve as convenient ways of outlining this discussion: First, there is the so-called Magisterial Reformation, the mainstream Protestant Reformation represented by Martin Luther, Ulrich Zwingli, and John Calvin. The second segment consists of some leading Roman Catholic theologians from the time of the Reformation, such as Ignatius of Loyola, John of Avila, and John of the Cross. Formerly named the Counter-Reformation—from the perspective of the Protestant Reformation—it is better to speak of the Catholic Reformation. Third, the pneumatologies of some Radical Reformers will be considered; representative leaders in this "left-wing" Protestant reformation were Thomas Müntzer and Menno Simons.

THE MAGISTERIAL REFORMERS ON THE SPIRIT

None of the Magisterial Reformers, namely, Martin Luther, John Calvin, and Ulrich Zwingli, considered the doctrine of the Holy Spirit to be a major issue of contention. This is not to say that there were no disputes either between them and Rome or among them (such as those between Luther and Zwingli) nor that the Reformers did not produce any distinctive pneumatologies. Rather it is to say that they owned the main creedal and Christian tradition[4] and delved into specific questions only to the extent that they were part of other theological loci, such as soteriology, ecclesiology, and the doctrine of revelation. In this light, the following statement by the leading Lutheran pneumatologist of the former generation is an overstatement:

> The concept of the Holy Spirit completely dominates Luther's theology. In every decisive matter, whether it be the study of Luther's doctrine of justification, of his doctrine of the sacraments, of his ethics, or of any other fundamental teaching, we are forced to take into consideration this concept of the Holy Spirit.[5]

If that kind of statement would apply to any of the Reformers, Calvin would be the most likely candidate.

The Life-Giving and Sanctifying Spirit

In keeping with tradition, Calvin saw the Bible, particularly in Romans 8, as teaching that while the Father is the fountain and source of everything, and the Son, the wisdom and order of the world, the "energy and efficacy of action is assigned to the Spirit." This, in turn, led him to affirm filioque. In the divine taxonomy, the Father, first in order, can never be without his wisdom (Son), second in order, and energy (Spirit), third in order—who derives from both of them.[6]

Similarly to Augustine and Christian tradition in general, Luther related the designation *Holy* Spirit to the Spirit's most distinctive work, that of sanctification. In the third article's reference to sanctification, "is expressed and portrayed the Holy Spirit and his office, which is that he makes us holy. Therefore, we must concentrate on the term 'Holy Spirit,' because it is so precise that we can find no substitute for it." The Spirit's work in sanctification corresponds to the Father's work in creation and the Son's in redemption. Luther also tells us the locus of the Spirit's sanctifying work: "The Holy Spirit effects our sanctification through . . . the communion of saints or Christian church, the forgiveness of sins, the resurrection of the body, and the life everlasting. In other words, he first leads us into his holy community, placing us upon the bosom of the church, where he preaches to us and brings us to Christ."[7] Indeed, for Luther, as in the ancient Christian tradition, the church is our mother who gives birth and nurtures us through the Word in the Holy Spirit.[8]

While sticking with tradition, Reformation theologians' creativity helped produce new metaphors, symbols, and analogies of the Spirit. Taking his clue from the saying in Acts 17:28 according to which "in him we live and move and have our being," Luther came up with the idea of calling the Father the "substance" of the Godhead; the Son, the "motion" or "movement," having been sent by the Father; and the Spirit, the "rest": "We live according to the Spirit, in whom the Father and the Son rest and live, as it were."[9] In explaining the meaning of the "Paraclete" in John 14–16, Luther compared the Spirit's role to that of the preacher who, in the analogy of an excellent pastor, reminds the congregation of the dangers of false teachers and of those who boast in human merits. The Holy Spirit sets the example by speaking on Christ's authority rather than on his own. The Holy Spirit takes from Christ's own and shares that with us rather than delivering a "human dream and thought."[10] In keeping with the ancient rule of *lex orandi, lex credendi*, Calvin found a number of names for the Holy Spirit illustrative of the Spirit's work in salvation, such as the "Spirit of adoption," "Water," "Oil" or "Unction," "Fire," "Fountain," and so forth.[11]

The traditional linking of the Holy Spirit with the work of sanctification in the church did not cause the Reformers to lose sight of the presence of the Spirit in the world and created order. Luther's *Lectures on Genesis* finds a delightful way of presenting the creative work of the Spirit. He names the Holy Spirit the hen who broods her eggs and keeps them warm in order to have them hatch. This is another way of speaking of "the office of the Holy Spirit [which is] to make alive."[12] Calvin, whose theology at large lends to a cosmic, creation-affirmative outlook, uses the biblical teaching on the universal presence of the Spirit in the world as one of the ways to affirm the deity of the Spirit. Indeed, the Genevan Reformer says it is "by no means an obscure testimony which Moses bears in the history of the creation, when he says that the Spirit of God was expanded over the abyss or shapeless matter."[13] In his *Commentary on Psalms* Calvin speaks of the Spirit's role in creation in a way that has a close affinity with contemporary theologies' stress on the Spirit as the principle of life:

> We continue to live, so long as he sustains us by his power; but no sooner does he withdraw his life-giving spirit than we die. Even Plato knew this, who so often teaches that, properly speaking, there is but one God, and that all things subsist, or have their being only in him. . . . He [the Psalmist] again declares, that the world is daily *renewed*, because *God sends forth his spirit*. In the propagation of living creatures, we doubtless see continually a new creation of the world. In now calling *that* God's spirit, which he before

> represented as the spirit of living creatures, there is no contradiction. God
> sendeth forth that spirit which remains with him whither he pleases; and as
> soon as he has sent it forth, all things are created. In this way, what was his
> own he makes to be ours. . . . Since then the world daily dies, and is daily
> renewed in its various parts, the manifest conclusion is, that it subsists only
> by a secret virtue derived from God.[14]

What makes Calvin's talk about the cosmic, creative work of the Spirit in
creation so remarkable in terms of contemporary holistic tendencies is his linking the creative work to the regenerative work in salvation. Having spoken of
the Spirit's "being diffused over all space, sustaining, invigorating, and quickening all things, both in heaven and on the earth," he lifts up the Spirit's work in
"regeneration to incorruptible life" as a work higher and "much more excellent
than any present quickening." In all of this, Calvin sees the supremacy of the
Spirit's work in creation and new creation.[15]

The Spirit, the Word, and Sacraments

The title for chapter 7 in the first book of the *Institutes* illustrates a leading theme
in Calvin's theology of revelation: "The Testimony of the Spirit Necessary to
Give Full Authority to Scripture." Here Calvin sets his Protestant view in opposition with the Catholic doctrine of Scripture, in which the ultimate authority of
the Bible rests on the church, by setting forth his own pneumatological understanding of the biblical authority:

> Our conviction of the truth of Scripture must be derived from a higher
> source than human conjectures, judgments, or reasons; namely, the secret
> testimony of the Spirit. . . . The testimony of the Spirit is superior to rea-
> son. For as God alone can properly bear witness to his own words, so these
> words will not obtain full credit in the hearts of men, until they are sealed
> by the inward testimony of the Spirit. The same Spirit, therefore, who
> spoke by the mouth of the prophets, must penetrate our hearts, in order to
> convince us that they faithfully delivered the message with which they were
> divinely entrusted.[16]

Zwingli affirms the same truth in his *Defense of the Reformed Faith*.[17] Hence, the
saving power of Scripture is the function of the authority of God brought about
by the Holy Spirit.[18]

Consequently, the Reformers insisted on the necessity of the Holy Spirit
as the key to understanding the written word of Scripture. In his exposition
on the Magnificat, Luther used Mary as the paradigm of a Christian who is
"enlightened and instructed by the Holy Spirit." Indeed, Luther continues,
"No one can correctly understand God or His Word unless he has received
such understanding immediately from the Holy Spirit."[19] The fact that the
understanding can be received immediately, however, does not mean laziness
in the study of Scripture; rather, Luther reminds us, again as a lesson from

the Mother of Jesus, that "no one can receive it from the Holy Spirit without experiencing, proving, and feeling it" because in "such experience the Holy Spirit instructs us as in His own school, outside of which nothing is learned but empty words and prattle."[20]

The insistence on the inner testimony of the Spirit, with Roman Catholics in view, however, does not mean opening the door for those whom the Reformers called "Enthusiasts." Indeed, their view is rebutted as vehemently as that of Rome. The Spirit's saving work is tied to the Word; this truth Calvin saw highlighted, for example, in 2 Corinthians 3:8:

> There is nothing repugnant here to what was lately said (chap. 7) that we have no great certainty of the word itself, until it be confirmed by the testimony of the Spirit. For the Lord has so knit together the certainty of his word and his Spirit, that our minds are duly imbued with reverence for the word when the Spirit shining upon it enables us there to behold the face of God; and, on the other hand, we embrace the Spirit with no danger of delusion when we recognise him in his image, that is, in his word.[21]

Luther, similarly, was greatly concerned about the danger among the Enthusiasts to sever the Spirit from the Word. In his perception, the Anabaptists and others who thought similarly relied on direct revelations and unmediated faith. Luther spoke of two "sendings" of the Holy Spirit: in the miraculous events of the primitive church and in the coming of the Spirit as the preached Word into the hearts of the believers. The "visible" sending of the Spirit in the New Testament—first in the form of the dove at Jesus' baptism and then through visible signs in the early church—were necessary as long as the church had been properly gathered. This visible sending gave way to the "invisible" one,

> that by which the Holy Spirit, through the Word, is sent into the hearts of believers, as is said here: "God has sent the Spirit of His Son into your hearts." This happens without a visible form, that is, when through the spoken Word we receive fire and light, by which we are made new and different, and by which a new judgment, new sensations, and new drives arise in us. This change and new judgment are not the work of human reason or power; they are the gift and accomplishment of the Holy Spirit, who comes with the preached Word, purifies our hearts by faith, and produces spiritual motivation in us.[22]

The way Calvin expresses the integrated work of the Word and Spirit is to speak of a twofold work of God, "inwardly, by his Spirit; outwardly, by his Word."[23]

The surest and the most reliable way for the Spirit to work in tandem with the Word is, in the opinion of Luther, tied to the sacraments. Indeed, at times Luther saw it necessary to emphasize the relation of the Spirit and Word to sacraments so much so that he denied any possibility of the reception of Spirit apart from them: "Accordingly, we should and must constantly maintain that God will not deal with us except through his external Word and sacrament. Whatever is attributed to the Spirit apart from such Word and sacrament is of the devil." This is the safeguard against Thomas Müntzer, a leader in the Radical Reformation, and those like him.[24] The church's main task, then, is to preach Christ in order for the "Holy Spirit to create, call, and gather the Christian church."[25]

Not only with regard to salvation but also in relation to any kind of authority, it is necessary to link the Spirit with the Word, as Zwingli explains: "Whether the Spirit of God is with you is demonstrated above all, by whether his word is your guide, and by whether you do nothing except what is clearly stated in the word of God so that scripture is your master and not you, masters of scripture."[26] Consequently, the best way to be assured of the discernment of God's will is to "give heed to the word" because that is the only way that "we acquire pure and clear knowledge of the will of God and are drawn to him by his Spirit and transformed into his likeness."[27] Luther saw in this a great source of comfort: unlike the "sectarians" who "imagine that God comforts us immediately, without His word," in distress the believer can be assured of the comfort of the Spirit that comes from the Word.[28]

The stress on the relation of the Spirit to the Word (and sacraments) meant that, by and large, the Magisterial Reformers preferred to speak of the fruit of the Spirit[29] over the charismatic gifts. It is easy to understand why: both the Anabaptists and Roman Catholics often elevated the role of healings, prophecies, visions, and other charisms above the Word and sacraments; at least that was the perception of Luther and Calvin. While cautious about the charismatic gifts, in his commentary on Joel 2:28,[30] Calvin acknowledges that with the coming of Christ there is an increase of gifts when compared to the time of the prophets. Indeed, in the New Testament, the promise of the outpouring of the Spirit is "upon all flesh." In his commentary on 1 Corinthians 12:4–7, Calvin offers a number of remarks on the role of spiritual gifts in the service of the upbuilding of the church.

The Spirit's Work in Salvation

One of the most familiar phrases to all Lutherans summarizes well the necessary role of the Holy Spirit with regard to salvation:

> I believe that by my own reason or strength I cannot believe in Jesus Christ, my Lord, or come to him. But the Holy Spirit has called me through the Gospel, enlightened me with his gifts, and sanctified and preserved me in true faith, just as he calls, gathers, enlightens, and sanctifies the whole Christian church on earth and preserves it in union with Jesus Christ in the one true faith.[31]

Similar statements can also be found in Zwingli's writings.[32]

Both Luther and Calvin referred to St. Augustine in their theology of the Spirit and salvation. With reference to the bishop of Hippo, Calvin reminds us of the fact that the Holy Spirit's necessary instrumental role in turning the heart of the elect to God does not mean the passivity of the renewed will. He affirms the Augustinian teaching that the "agency of man is not destroyed by the motion of the Holy Spirit, because nature furnishes the will which is guided so as to aspire to good." Rather, the human will is repaired by grace. Then, and only then, can it be said that "our will does what the Spirit does in us, although the will contributes nothing of itself apart from grace."[33]

While it is customary to describe the Protestant understanding of justification as a "forensic declaration," meaning that God pronounces the sinner righteous, it is also true that both Luther's own theology[34] (unlike Lutheran confessional writings owing to Melanchthon) and that of Calvin also operate with the idea of union between Christ and the believer. In this conception of justification, the Holy Spirit's role is much more pronounced. In the words of Calvin:

> To communicate to us the blessings which he received from the Father, he [Christ] must become ours and dwell in us. . . . We are said to be ingrafted into him and clothed with him, all which he possesses being, as I have said, nothing to us until we become one with him. And . . . since we see that all do not indiscriminately embrace the offer of Christ which is made by the gospel, the very nature of the case teaches us to ascend higher, and inquire into the secret efficacy of the Spirit, to which it is owing that we enjoy Christ and all his blessings. . . . Let us at present attend to the special point, that Christ came by water and blood, as the Spirit testifies concerning him. . . . It is not without cause that the testimony of the Spirit is . . . mentioned, a testimony which is engraven on our hearts by way of seal, and thus seals the cleansing and sacrifice of Christ. For which reason, also, Peter says, that believers are "elect" "through sanctification of the Spirit, unto obedience and sprinkling of the blood of Jesus Christ," (1 Pet. 1:2). By these words he reminds us, that if the shedding of his sacred blood is not to be in vain, our souls must be washed in it by the secret cleansing of the Holy Spirit.[35]

Zwingli's thirteenth article of the Reformed faith explains salvation by faith in a way that sounds quite surprising to Protestant formulations, namely, in terms of deification, an idea not unknown to Luther or Calvin but a formulation usually not found in Reformation tradition: "That a person is drawn to God by God's Spirit and deified, becomes quite clear from scripture . . . 'And when the Spirit of truth comes, he shall teach all truth,' Jn. 16.13."[36]

The same Holy Spirit is also the source of the testimony of belonging to Christ, as Luther explains in his comments on Romans 8:16. According to Luther this testimony consists of three parts: first, assurance of remission of sins because of God's kindness; second, assurance of the possibility of good works because of God's working in us; and third, assurance that the Spirit rather than the human being is behind all of this work, including eternal life.[37]

Against what Zwingli believes are Catholic suspicions about the lack of emphasis on good works in Reformed insistence on faith as the root of the Christian life, Zwingli saw it important to underline the importance of good works in terms of Christ's presence in the believer and the fruit of the Spirit: "The testament of the gospel is inscribed upon human hearts and works in us by the Spirit of God. From this follows: Where there is faith, there the Spirit of God is also, and where he is, there one may find good works."[38]

The same Spirit also strengthens and encourages Christians in need. The Spirit "groans" and prays for Christians even when, in their distress, they do not know how to. While the work of God is often hidden—as Luther often remarked in the context of his theology of the cross—Christians have no reason to lose hope. Luther saw here a wonderful source of encouragement and consolation.[39]

The Spirit in the Sacraments

One of the main disputes among the Reformers was related to sacraments in general and the Lord's Supper in particular. While discussion of those issues lies outside the parameters of this book, we will touch on some key pneumatological underpinnings. Among the Protestant Reformers, Luther's understanding was closest to the classic Catholic understanding even though he was reluctant to use the ancient term *ex opera operato*, which teaches that the effect of the sacrament is intact regardless of the conditions of either the administrator or the receiver (other than that the latter does not place a conscious obstacle in the way of reception). Luther's main concern was the close connection of the sacraments with the Word and Spirit, as discussed above.

On the other end of the Magisterial Reformation with regard to the topic of sacraments is Zwingli, who represents the "thinnest" sacramental understanding. While the term "symbolic" with reference to his view of the Lord's Supper may not be the most adequate one, it contains the kernel of truth that the Zurich Reformer was wary of the kind of "thick" sacramentalism that in his perception assigned to sacraments the main efficacy of the act.[40] Thus it is no wonder that he saw it necessary to revisit St. Augustine, who was the first to establish the classic sacramental teaching according to which the sacrament brings about what it promises. In critical engagement with Augustine's teaching in *On the Trinity* 15.26, Zwingli has this to say of the role of the Spirit in sacraments and the primacy of faith over the rite:

> In this passage of Augustine we have to consider three things. First, since he says that the Holy Ghost was not given by the disciples, that they only prayed for it, much less is it true that the bestowal of the Holy Ghost is bound up with the sacraments administered by the clergy. Secondly, that the bestowal of the Holy Ghost was not bound up with the laying on of hands, which I do not deny is a sacrament. For since they only prayed that the Holy Ghost might be given to those upon whom they laid hands, they had no power to promise this by laying on of hands. Finally, when Augustine says, "In which preeminently the baptized receive the Holy Ghost," he is speaking symbolically. . . . Thus receiving the Holy Ghost is not the effect of baptism, but baptism is the effect of having received the Holy Ghost. . . . For Augustine's remark that Christ received the Holy Ghost before His baptism, and that the apostles do not give the Holy Ghost, shows that there is no intimate connection of the Holy Ghost with the minister or the sacra-

ment. From this it follows at once that the language is used symbolically and not in its simple sense when that which belongs to the Spirit is attributed to the sacraments. And this will be made plainer by the second quotation.[41]

Over against sacramental theology, Zwingli wants to lessen the value of the sacrament itself (in this case the Eucharist) by arguing that it is faith that determines the spiritual effects:

> Although the gift and bounty of the divine goodness are extolled therein [in the Eucharist], they are not brought to us by the power of the symbols, except in so far as the symbols and the words of the preacher proclaim them. For it is alone the Spirit that draws the mind to that fountain by which the soul, that has pined away through despair over its sins, is refreshed and renewed in youth.

In other words, the "externals can do nothing more than proclaim and represent." Thus, Zwingli's conclusion is that "since faith is a gift of the Holy Spirit, it is clear that the Spirit operated before the external symbols were introduced."[42]

Calvin's understanding of the sacraments locates itself between the two other Reformation views, closer to Luther's in many ways. One of the long-lasting contributions of the Geneva Reformer lies in the pneumatological framing of the sacraments. The sacramental act is a pneumatological act in that "the sacraments duly perform their office only when accompanied by the Spirit, the internal Master, whose energy alone penetrates the heart, stirs up the affections, and procures access for the sacraments into our souls." The Holy Spirit is the real administrator of the sacramental act, and therefore, its effects or lack thereof are solely determined by the same Spirit.[43]

THE SPIRIT IN THE ROMAN CATHOLIC REFORMATION

> In the midst of my accustomed prayer, without deliberations, while offering or asking God our Lord that the oblation made be accepted by his Divine Majesty, I had abundant devotion and tears. Later, speaking with the Holy Spirit in view of saying his Mass, with the same devotion or tears I seemed to see him or perceive him in dense brightness or in the color of a flame of fire burning in an unusual way.
>
> A little later still when I was about to leave for Mass, while giving myself to a short prayer, I experienced an intense devotion, and tears came over me as I somehow perceived interiorly or saw the Holy Spirit. This, so to speak, made the election seem a finished matter. And yet I was unable to see either of the other two divine Persons.[44]

These two personal experiences as narrated by Ignatius of Loyola in his *Spiritual Diary* illustrate the importance of a deep spiritual experience. Ironically, the heyday of the Protestant Reformation, the year 1521, happened to be his time of conversion and dedication to the service of God and the Catholic Church. In keeping with the Catholic tradition, his spirituality and pneumatology are thoroughly

Trinitarian. At one point, having finished Mass and about to leave the church, he recalls that "during my prayer at the altar there was so much sobbing and effusion of tears, all terminating in the love of the Holy Trinity, that I seemed to have no desire to leave. For I was feeling so much love and so much spiritual sweetness."[45]

Catholic Reformers, in a way reminiscent of the practitioners of Orthodox spiritual exercises, were not afraid to give detailed instructions on how to prepare for the reception and ministry of the Spirit. John of Avila, in his collection of sermons *The Holy Ghost*, says that indeed no spiritual lesson is more important for the congregation than speaking of a proper preparation.[46] The guidelines include "that we should be aware of His power, and that we should believe that He can accomplish marvels" and that we have "the will to receive Him as our guest, sincerely and anxiously to desire His coming."[47] Renouncing sins such as concupiscence and other forms of sensuality is a proper way to honor the Holy Ghost, whose symbol is the dove, and concentrating on prayer and fasting are high on Avila's list of spiritual exercises.[48]

Following St. Paul—and again reflecting the spirituality of the Christian East as well—John of Avila makes the possession of the Spirit the hallmark of being a Christian: "'He who has not the Spirit of Christ is none of His.'. . . He who lives by his own spirit, does not belong to Christ. You are not to live according to your own intellect, your own will, or your own judgment; you are to live in the Spirit of Christ. You must have received the Spirit of Christ." But to live in the Spirit is nothing else than living in Christ: "What does the Spirit of Christ mean? The heart of Christ. He who does not possess the heart of Christ, does not belong to Christ."[49]

While sharp in their thinking, several Catholic Reformers were also drawn to mysticism of the Spirit. Part of the mystical texture is the vision of union between the divine and human by virtue of the work of the Spirit. The "Mystical Doctor," John of the Cross, the spiritual director of the "discalced" (barefoot, because they did not wear shoes) Carmelite Order was a leading mystical Catholic writer who alongside his closest spiritual colleague, Teresa of Avila, brought about a spiritual reform in the latter part of the sixteenth century. In his work with a telling title, *The Living Flame of Love*, he uses several metaphors when speaking of the union, such as fire, which "having entered wood, may have transformed it into itself and may be now united with it, but as the fire burns more intensely and is in it longer, the wood becomes increasingly more incandescent and inflamed until it flashes fire and sends out tongues of flame."[50] The first stanza of this work and its explanation elaborates on the work of the Holy Spirit in union.

> O living flame of love
> that tenderly wounds
> my soul in its deepest center; now that you are not contrary, finish then if
>   you wish,
> rend the veil of this sweet encounter!

1. The soul now feels itself completely inflamed in divine union, its palate now bathed in glory and love. Flowing forth no less than rivers of glory from even the most intimate part of its being, abounding now in joys, the soul feels flow *from its womb rivers of living water* which the Son of God said would flow forth in such souls. It seems to it that it is so close to blessedness that only a thin veil separates it, by such intensity is it transformed in God, so sublimely is it possessed by Him, and with such sumptuous wealth of gifts and virtues is it adorned. And it sees that each time that delicate flame of love which burns in it assails it, the flame does so as though it were glorifying the soul with gentle and powerful glory. This occurs to such a degree that each time the flame absorbs the soul and assails it, it seems that is going to give the soul eternal life and is going to tear the veil of mortal life, very little lacking. Due to that little, it has not yet completely been glorified in its substance. The soul therefore now says with great desire to the flame— which is the Holy Spirit—to rend mortal life through that sweet encounter, in which the flame truly communicates to the soul what it seems each time to be going to give to it and do when it encounters it, which is to glorify it entirely and perfectly. And so, the soul says: O living flame of love![51]

As any mystic, John of the Cross reminds us that it is only through love that the Spirit helps us be united with God. And the deeper the love, the deeper the union.[52] Part of the mystical approach is the freedom to use metaphors and symbols that are not directly drawn from the Bible but have affinity with biblical allusions. One of those metaphors is that of the "spice of wine":

This spiced wine is another much greater favor which God sometimes grants to advanced souls, in which He inebriates them in the Holy Spirit with a wine of sweet, delightful, and fortified love. Accordingly, she calls this love, "spiced wine." As this wine is seasoned and strengthened with many diverse, fragrant, and fortified spices, so this love, which God accords to those who are already perfect, is fermented and established in them and spiced with the virtues they have gained. Prepared with these precious spices, this wine gives such strength and abundance of sweet inebriation in these visits granted by God to the soul that they cause her to direct toward Him, efficaciously and forcefully, flowings or outpourings of praise, love, and reverence, etc., which we have mentioned. And she does this with admirable desires to work and suffer for Him.[53]

THE RADICAL REFORMERS ON THE SPIRIT

The Anabaptists and other Radical Reformers considered the reforms of mainline Protestantism wanting and desired to go further with the reform and renewal. While the umbrella term "Radical Reformation" is just that, an umbrella that covers various types of reform movements, from politically active to neutral or from highly charismatic and prophetic to more ethically and discipleship-oriented ones, it is also a helpful nomenclature to distinguish that group from Roman Catholics, Magisterial Reformers, and British (or Anglican) Reformers.

Present at the famous disputation between Luther and Johann Eck in 1519 and at times quite close to Luther, Thomas Müntzer drifted away from both

Luther and his theology and started advocating a sectarian, pneumatic understanding of theology and church. Like any spiritual reformer, Müntzer assumed great spiritual authority to himself and, as a consequence, took the right to harshly criticize the teachers of the church, both past and contemporary, for skewed interpretation of the Bible and doctrines. Rightly or wrongly, he and other Radicals were accused by mainline Reformers of emphasizing the "inner word" and hearing directly from the Spirit at the expense of the written word. Some of their statements give rise to this kind of suspicion:

> Hence Paul [is] . . . speaking there [in Romans 10] of the inward word which is to be heard in the abyss of the soul through the revelation of God. Now anyone who has not become conscious and receptive to this through the living witness of God, Romans 8, may have devoured a hundred thousand Bibles, but he can say nothing about God which has any validity. . . . The holy spirit must direct him to consider earnestly the pure and straight-forward meaning of the law, Psalm 18. Otherwise his heart will be blind and he will dream up for himself a wooden Christ and lead himself astray. . . . Similarly, if a man is to receive the revelation of God he must cut himself off from all distractions and develop an earnest concern for the truth. . . .[54]

One of the complaints of Radical Reformers is the lack of true, genuine faith in the life of most Christians and instead a shallow, formal reliance on human traditions and rites. In his *On Counterfeit Faith*, Müntzer calls for sincere repentance and personal faith.[55] Similarly, another key leader, Menno Simons—whose followers became known as Mennonites (*Mennisten*)—showed constant concern that people who called themselves Christians were not truly newborn. He sounded a strong call for sincere repentance, personal experience of new birth, and submission of one's life to wholehearted devotion of discipleship and suffering, ideas that are powerfully presented in his *New Birth*.[56]

Unlike some of his colleagues, Menno Simons also took pains to demonstrate his alignment with received tradition, such as that of the Trinitarian doctrine and the Spirit's role therein. The title of his work clearly reveals this purpose: *A Solemn Confession of the Triune, Eternal, and True God, Father, Son, and Holy Ghost*.[57] Menno also took pains in his apologetic writings to defend himself against accusations concerning the alleged departure from tradition:

> I never entertained the thought that God's Holy and eternal Spirit was not God in God, and God with God. Yet, Gellius would accuse us, who are not guilty, of denying the sanctification, grace, fruit, and power of the Holy Spirit, because some, who have been expelled by us, have erred in this respect, and probably still err; although he sees with his eyes and feels with his hands the sanctification and power of the Holy Spirit in our people.[58]

Chapter 5

Post-Reformation
and Modern Pneumatologies

Roughly speaking, two main orientations to pneumatology emerged in the aftermath of the Reformation and during the ensuing years until the eve of the twentieth century, namely, Protestant scholasticism (or Protestant orthodoxy) and various revival and renewal movements. The term *Protestant scholasticism* or *orthodoxy* usually refers to the seventeenth- and eighteenth-century Lutheran[1] and Reformed[2] theologies, which took pains in formulating Christian doctrines in a most meticulous and articulated way. Often it was done in debate with Roman Catholic doctrines and traditions. Similarly to their medieval forebears, Aristotelian logic and philosophical argumentation—coupled with careful biblical study and the use of ancient sources—provided the tools of the trade. The Lutheran Johann Gerhard's massive nine-volume *Loci Theologicae* ("Theological Topics") and the Reformed Francis Turretin's almost 2,000-page-long *Institutio Theologiae Elencticae* ("Institutes of Elenctic Theology") are the greatest examples of this genre.

Speaking of a number of Protestant renewal movements that arose in the aftermath of the Reformation, such as Puritanism, Pietism, holiness movements, and evangelicalism, Donald Bloesch gives an apt description:

A burgeoning interest in the spiritual life is reflected in the rise of movements of spiritual purification after the Reformation in the late sixteenth through the nineteenth and early twentieth centuries. . . . These are convergent rather than divergent currents of renewal, and they often overlap. Yet each one has distinctive emphases, and this is why I treat them separately. Though emerging in the past they continue in new forms. A common strand in all these movements is the emphasis on heart religion. It is not enough to subscribe to the tenets of the faith. One must have a palpable experience of the object of faith if one is to be regarded as a true believer. A purely theoretical knowledge of Christ must give way to an existential knowledge, often called the knowledge of acquaintance. Many of these people manifested an appreciation for the mystics of the faith, though they generally steered clear of mystics who gravitated toward pantheism. The need to prepare the heart for the gift of grace as well as the role of disciplines of devotion that enable us to remain in the state of grace are also conspicuous in these ventures of renewal. The Puritans, Pietists and Evangelicals were united in affirming the Reformation doctrine of salvation by grace alone (*sola gratia*) and justification by faith alone (*sola fide*), though they wished to unite these themes with the biblical call to holiness. An exclusive emphasis on faith alone was treated with grave reservations by many of the revival leaders, including John Wesley. Faith must prove itself in a life of outgoing love.[3]

The Wesleyan brothers and Methodism, the Great Awakening pioneers of the eighteenth and nineteenth centuries in Wales and in the United States, as well as the Quakers, are other examples of renewal movements owing to the Reformation that will be discussed under the wide umbrella concept of post-Reformation renewal movements. These movements can be conveniently called the "religion of the heart."

PROTESTANT SCHOLASTICS

The main loci for the Protestant scholastics to discuss the Holy Spirit in dogmatic presentations had to do with the inspiration and authority of Scripture, the Trinity, the *ordo salutis* (the subjective reception of salvation wrought about by the objective work of Christ), and means of grace, particularly the sacraments, as well as some other ecclesiological topics.[4]

The deity and "personhood" of the Spirit is "proved" from Scriptural passages, and the divine attributes such as eternity ascribed to the Holy Spirit in Scripture.[5] Filioque is affirmed on the basis of Western tradition and Augustine.[6]

Everything in Scripture is inspired by the Holy Spirit.[7] At times, the way inspiration is attributed to the Holy Spirit is almost mechanical, such as the formulation by D. Hollaz:

I. The conceptions of all that is contained in the Holy Scriptures were immediately communicated by the Holy Spirit to the prophets and apostles.

II. All the words, without exception, contained in the Holy Manuscript, were dictated by the Holy Spirit to the pen of the prophets and apostles.[8]

The same Holy Spirit affects the "internal witness of the Holy Spirit" related to the witness of the spirit of sonship.[9] Heinrich Heppe, in summarizing the Reformed view, goes so far as to say that the reason "all Reformed dogmaticians are in essential agreement" about the "knowability of its [Scripture's] divineness and inspiration" is "the *testimonium Spiritus sancti* as the real proof."[10]

In keeping with Protestant theology in general, scholastic theology discusses the "subjective" reception of salvation (*ordo salutis*) under pneumatology: "Of the Grace of the Holy Spirit in the Application of Redemption."[11] Having first explained that salvation is a Trinitarian event, Hollaz offers this explanation of the role of the Holy Spirit:

> The *applying grace of the Holy Spirit is the source* of those divine acts by which the Holy Spirit, through the Word of God and the Sacraments, dispenses, offers to us, bestows and seals the spiritual and eternal favors designed for many by the great mercy of God the Father, and procured by the fraternal redemption of Jesus Christ.[12]

One of the topics widely discussed and debated particularly by the Lutheran Scholastics had to do with the relationship between human will and the agency of the Holy Spirit. In other words, what is the agency of the Holy Spirit in moving the human will toward God?[13] On the Reformed side, this discussion takes place in the context of election and calling: according to that tradition, the call by the Holy Spirit is given only to the elect: "Without this activity of the Holy Spirit, who writes the Word in man's heart, God's Word itself is but an empty letter."[14]

The Holy Spirit helps apply the great benefits of salvation—such as faith, justification, call, illumination, regeneration and conversion, mystical union, renovation, and good works—through the means of grace, the Word and sacraments. In the sacraments, "as in the case of the Word . . . an external and visible element . . . becomes the vehicle of the Holy Ghost."[15] Put in a technical language, with regard to the sacrament of baptism, "*the heavenly object of Baptism is analogically called the whole sacred Trinity, but peculiarly and terminatively the Holy Spirit.*"[16]

Whereas scholastic Protestant theology aimed at carefully delineated doctrinal formulas with the help of theological and philosophical argumentation, several other post-Reformation movements, while not leaving behind the desire to analyze as carefully as possible pneumatological topics, had their main focus on the life lived in the Spirit—in other words, in the spirituality and renewal of the Holy Spirit. To these testimonies we turn next.

RENEWAL MOVEMENTS: THE "RELIGION OF THE HEART"

Puritanism

The Puritanists formed a significant renewal movement within or originating in Anglicanism. Unlike some other Protestant Reformation movements, Puritans not only emphasized the "heart faith" but also the role of sacraments and rites. Some leading Puritanists, such as John Owen and Thomas Goodwin, were shapers of the Congregationalist wing of Puritanism.

Richard Sibbes, a priest in the Church of England, was one of the greatest Puritans of the first generation at the turn of the seventeenth century, and his influence was felt all over the English-speaking world beyond his own church. In keeping with Puritanist spirituality, he spoke extensively of the role of the Spirit in salvation and life of the Christian. Commenting on 2 Corinthians 3:17 ("Now the Lord is that Spirit: and where the Spirit of the Lord is, there is liberty"), Sibbes formulates a thick Spirit-Christology as the basis of soteriology: "'The Lord is that Spirit' that takes away the veil that is spoken of before. He sets down what Christ is by what he doth; Christ is 'that Spirit,' because he gives the Spirit. And then a sweet effect of the Spirit of Christ, 'Where the Spirit of Christ is, there is liberty.'"[17] Consequently, Christ is the one who dispenses the Spirit to others, and conversely, "all [are] receiving the Spirit from him as the common root and fountain of all spiritual gifts." The soteriological implication of this robust Spirit-Christology is that whatever the Father is doing in the life of the Son through his Spirit is being given to us in Christ through the Spirit.[18]

No wonder Sibbes makes the possession of the Spirit the hallmark of being a Christian; he is of course following no one else but St. Paul:

> Briefly, a man may know that he is in Christ, if he find the Spirit of Christ in him; for the same Spirit when Christ took our nature, that sanctified that blessed mass whereof he was made, when there was a union between him and the second person, the same Spirit sanctifies our souls and bodies. There is one Spirit in the head and in the members. Therefore if we find the Spirit of Christ in us, we are in Christ and he in us.[19]

In keeping with the renewal spirituality, exhortations with regard to not quenching the Spirit can be found in Sibbes, similarly to many of his colleagues.[20] A passionate preacher, Sibbes issues particularly serious warnings to those who are about to miss the call of the gospel to repent, communicated through the Spirit: "Oh, do not resist these holy stirrings within you; give way to the motions of the blessed Spirit of God; second them with holy resolutions to practise the same; let them sink deep into your hearts, root them there."[21] To put it the other way, a positive response to the call of the gospel is to desire the Spirit and the Spirit's blessings.[22]

Widely considered the most significant Puritan alongside John Edwards, John Owen wore many hats: that of the pastor, chaplain to Oliver Cromwell, vice-chancellor of Oxford University, and finally the leader for the Independents. The title of a widely used devotional work, *Of Communion with God the Father, Son and Holy Ghost*, is an indication of a masterful blending of homily, exhortation, and doctrinal acumen. While communion and grace are gifts from the Father, Son, and Spirit, Owen surmises that the Father communicates grace with "original authority"; the Son, by way of communicating from a "purchased treasury"; and the Spirit does it by the way of "immediate efficacy."

Owen uses Romans 8:11 as a case in point: "Here is the Father's authoritative quickening,—'He raised Christ from the dead, and he shall quicken you;' and the Son's mediatory quickening,—for it is done in 'the death of Christ;' and the Spirit's immediate efficacy,—'He shall do it by the Spirit that dwelleth in you.'"[23] The most common designation for the Holy Spirit, in keeping with tradition, is "that he is given and received as of gift."[24]

In his main work on pneumatology, *A Discourse Concerning the Holy Spirit*—or briefly just *Pneumatologia*—Owen carefully steers a middle course between rationalistic approaches that tend to downplay spiritual experience and enthusiastic movements that place too much emphasis on the Spirit. Interestingly, Owen begins his study with the consideration of spiritual gifts, charisms. Typical of his orderly and logical treatment, he presents a full outline of the nature and purpose of charisms in the church.[25] Indicative of his inclusive and comprehensive doctrine of the Spirit, Owen's treatise includes even topics such as the Spirit's role in creation and providence. Following the ancient rule of *opera Trinitatis ad extra sunt indivisa* (the works of the Trinity outwardly are indivisible), he considers in detail the distinctions and unity of the work of the Trinity and then says of the Spirit's role,

> Whereas the *order of operation* among the distinct persons depends on the *order* of their subsistence in the blessed Trinity, in every great work of God, the *concluding, completing, perfecting acts* are ascribed unto the Holy Ghost. This we shall find in all the instances of them that will fall under our consideration. Hence, the immediate actings of the Spirit are the most hidden, curious, and mysterious, as those which contain the perfecting part of the works of God.[26]

It is clear without saying that in this great pneumatological treatise, Owen also considers in great detail the Spirit's role in various aspects of soteriology, including a careful discussion of the sanctifying work.

Other significant pneumatological contributions from the leading Puritanists came from the pen of Thomas Goodwin, who, with Owen, aligned himself with the Congregationalist wing. He is the author of the highly noteworthy *The Work of the Holy Ghost in Our Salvation*, a treasure house of pneumatology and soteriology.[27] While John Bunyan's *Spiritual Progress* may be the most widely used devotional classic, his *Grace Abounding to the Chief of Sinners*[28] is a profound personal testimony to his spiritual struggle with the constant fear of sinning against the Holy Spirit. Similarly, widely known are the works of the greatest English preacher, Charles Haddon Spurgeon. In a sermon titled "The Holy Ghost—The Great Teacher," Spurgeon, having lamented the state of spiritual knowledge in his times, argues for the necessity of the Holy Spirit as the Christian's guide and teacher, based on Jesus' promise of sending the Comforter:

> This generation hath gradually, and almost imperceptibly, become to a great extent a godless generation. . . . Even among professing Christians, while there is a great amount of religion, there is too little godliness: there

is much external formalism, but too little inward acknowledgment of God. In many places dedicated to Jehovah the name of Jesus is too often kept in the background; the Holy Spirit is almost entirely neglected; and very little is said concerning his sacred influence. . . . May God send us a Christ-exalting, Spirit-loving ministry—men who shall proclaim God the Holy Ghost in all his offices and shall extol God the Saviour as the author and finisher of our faith. . . . Now . . . we require a guide to conduct us into all truth. . . . This person is "he, the Spirit," the "Spirit of truth;" not an influence or an emanation, but actually a person. "When the Spirit of truth is come, he shall guide you into all truth."[29]

Pietism

Similarly to Puritanism, Pietism, Puritanism's counterpart among Lutheran and Reformed churches, continues to exercise its influence up to the present time. Unlike those who followed Protestant orthodoxy with its detailed schemes of *ordo salutis*, Pietists and Puritans considered personal faith, often termed new birth, as an experience to be sought. This is not to say that the renewal theologians were not theologians; rather it is to say that their stated desire and deep yearning of the heart was to have the experience of salvation along with the right understanding.

Routinely named the father of Pietism, Johann Arndt was both a staunch defender of Lutheran orthodoxy at the turn of the sixteenth century and a passionate preacher for a personal experience of faith—so much so that Albert Schweitzer in hindsight named him the "prophet of interior Protestantism."[30] In the classic work *True Christianity*, on the topic of "How man is once again renewed to eternal life in Christ," Arndt outlines what happens in new birth. New birth is the work of the Holy Spirit through faith, Word, and sacrament, a work "by which our heart, thoughts, mind, understanding, will, and affections are made holy, renewed, and enlightened as a new creature in and according to Jesus Christ. The new birth contains two chief aspects in itself: justification and sanctification or renewal (Tit. 3:5)."[31] As a result, the Christian has "two birth lines in himself," that of Adam and of Christ. A Lutheran theologian, Arndt further explains the renewing work of the Holy Spirit in tandem with that of Christ:

> The new birth in a spiritual manner is continued from Christ and this occurs through the Word of God. The Word of God is the seed of the new birth (1 Pet. 1:23; . . . Jas. 1:18 . . .). This Word awakens faith and faith clings to this Word and grasps in the Word Jesus Christ together with the Holy Spirit. Through the Holy Spirit's power and activity, man is new-born. The new birth occurs first through the Holy Spirit (John 3:4). This is what the Lord calls "to be born of the Spirit."[32]

Part of the texture of yearning for a "higher life" among Pietists is a mystical element and language regarding union with Christ. Arndt admires the three-fold "relationship, community, and union of the highest and eternal God" with human beings as established in the three works of grace, namely, the creation of human beings in God's image, the incarnation, and the sending of the Holy

Spirit. All of these works have as their ultimate goal "communion with God in which the highest and only blessedness of man consists."[33]

Highly mystical—often idiosyncratic[34]—is the theology and spirituality of Jacob Böhme, also known by the last name Behmen. A shoemaker by profession, he had a number of mystical experiences, including a significant spiritual vision in 1600 through which he claimed to have had the spiritual structure of the world revealed to him. Many of those visions were published in his first work, *Aurora*. Echoing the precepts of some Eastern Christian fathers and later mystics, Böhme claims that truly spiritual vision is available for spiritual people. It takes holiness to see the Holy God. A "carnal" Christian is hardly granted that kind of spiritual experience. Böhme asks the rhetorical question "Is then the Holy Spirit to be supposed blind when he dwells in man?"[35]

If Arndt is the father of Pietism, then Philip Jacob Spener is the movement's devotionalist. His *Pia Desideria* or "Heartfelt Desire for God-pleasing Reform" is the classic statement of Pietism and is often considered the birthmark of the movement. First published in 1675 by Spener, it is both a devotional work and a textbook on church renewal against the deadness and moral laxity of churches of the time. He deplores the spiritual state of too many preachers who in his estimation do ministry solely "with their own human efforts and without the working of the Holy Spirit." Even if they know the Scripture and the true doctrine, spiritual life and experience is missing.[36] In keeping with the "inner religion" of Pietism, Spener outlines "proposals for correcting conditions," as he puts it, especially regarding renewed preaching:

> Our whole Christian religion consists of the inner man or the new man, whose soul is faith and whose expressions are the fruits of life, and all sermons should be aimed at this. . . . Words should be so set in motion that we may by no means be content merely to have the people refrain from outward vices and practice outward virtues . . . but that we lay the right foundation in the heart, show that what does not proceed from this foundation is mere hypocrisy, and hence accustom the people first to work on what is inward (awaken love of God and neighbor through suitable means) and only then to act accordingly. One should therefore emphasize that the divine means of Word and sacrament are concerned with the inner man. Hence it is not enough that we hear the Word with our outward ear, but we must let it penetrate to our heart, so that we may hear the Holy Spirit speak there, that is, with vibrant emotion and comfort feel the sealing of the Spirit and the power of the Word.[37]

In the same vein, Nicholaus Ludwig Count von Zinzendorf, the leader of the Moravians, passionately called for the necessity of personal faith and the experience of new birth, particularly for those who are preachers and teachers of the church. Only those "disciples" who know how to pray rightly, who are born of the Holy Spirit, and know how to listen to their Father's voice will receive the true message of Christ.[38]

Among the nineteenth-century Pietists, none are so powerful in influence, provocative in their approach, and inclusive in their vision than the two Blumhardts, who along with Zinzendorf represent the Reformed side of the movement. The elder Blumhardt, Johann Christoph, was confronted in 1842 with a pastoral challenge: how to deal with one of his parishioners, a young woman by the name Gottlieben Dittus who suffered obviously from some disorder and was believed to have psychic visitations. Johann Christoph concluded she was demon possessed. The son of Johann Christoph, Christoph Friedrich, happened to be born right at the time his father was dealing with the young woman's demons. Having left the parish pastorate because of disillusionment with the church and academic theology, he became a well-known evangelist and faith healer. That career, however, came to an end in the aftermath of a successful crusade in Berlin in 1888 as Christoph concluded that it is not healing but cleansing that really matters in the Christian life. As a result of their unique spiritual and ministry paths, the Blumhardts became advocates of a highly inclusive vision of renewal in which the Holy Spirit was present not only in inspiration and salvation but also in charismatic empowerment, such as in the gift of healing as well as in sociopolitical improvement.[39]

Methodism

A former Anglican minister, John Wesley is the father of the Methodist movement, which has had worldwide influence and a focus on holiness and pursuit of perfection. Having returned to his homeland, England, from Savannah, Georgia, Wesley had the famous "heart strangely warmed" transformative spiritual experience at Aldersgate Street on May 24, 1738, which he shares in his journal.[40] That experience began a spiritual journey that had as its goal a deeper spiritual life beyond justification,[41] a perfection in love and holiness. With emphasis on holiness and renewal, Wesley was naturally drawn to consider carefully the role of the Holy Spirit in the Christian life. In his sermon "On the Holy Spirit," while taking for granted the existence and availability of at least some of the charismatic gifts of the apostolic church, Wesley sees the Spirit's main work in terms of "preparation for a life in God, which we are to enjoy hereafter. The gift of the Holy Spirit looks full to the resurrection; for then is the life of God completed in us." The final aim of the Christian life is the full bestowal of the Holy Spirit, "when the flesh shall no longer resist it, but be itself changed into an angelical condition, being clothed upon with the incorruption of the Holy Spirit; when the body which, by being born with the soul, and living through it, could only be called an animal one, shall now become spiritual, whilst by the Spirit it rises into eternity."[42]

While Wesley speaks of Christian perfection everywhere in his sermons, Bible expositions, and other places, the short tract *A Plain Account of Christian Perfection*, usually dated after its last revision in 1777, is the *locus classicus*. Often he describes perfection as perfect love, the pursuit of which consumed his life from early on, as the first brief citation from the beginning of the tract reveals: "In the beginning of the year 1738 . . . the cry of my heart was, O grant that nothing in my soul / May dwell, but thy pure love alone! / O may thy love possess me whole, / My joy, my treasure, and my crown! / Strange fires far from my heart remove; / My every act, word, thought, be love!"[43] With all his insistence on the possibility of reaching perfection, Wesley also granted the continuing struggle with sin in the life of the believer. This is the daily struggle between Spirit and flesh:

> "The flesh lusteth against the Spirit, and the Spirit against the flesh: These are contrary the one to the other." (Gal. 5:17) Nothing can be more express. The Apostle here directly affirms that the flesh, evil nature, opposes the Spirit, even in believers; that even in the regenerate there are two principles, "contrary the one to the other." . . . Indeed this grand point, that there are two contrary principles in believers,—nature and grace, the flesh and the Spirit, runs through all the epistles of St. Paul, yea, through all the Holy Scriptures.[44]

Swiss by birth, John Fletcher, a British Anglican priest, gave full support to Wesley's vision of perfection. Defining perfection in various ways, his main choice, similarly, was perfection in love:

> Christian perfection is a spiritual constellation made up of these gracious stars: perfect repentance, perfect faith, perfect humility, perfect meekness, perfect self-denial, perfect resignation, perfect hope, perfect charity for our visible enemies (as well as for our earthly relations) and above all, perfect love for our invisible God, through the explicit knowledge of our Mediator Jesus Christ. As this last star is always accompanied by all the others, as Jupiter is by his satellites, we frequently use (as St. John) the phrase *perfect love* instead of the word *perfection*. We understand by it the pure love of God shed abroad in the heart of established believers by the Holy Ghost, which is abundantly given them under the fullness of the Christian dispensation.[45]

The English preacher of Calvinist orientation of the American "Great Awakening," George Whitefield, considered to be another founder of Methodism along with the Wesley brothers, is best known for his powerful sermons. This great evangelist says that "walking with God" means nothing less than that "the prevailing power of the enmity of a person's heart be taken away by the blessed Spirit of God."[46] In a remarkable sermon titled "The Indwelling of the Spirit, the Common Privilege of All Believers," the evangelist attempts passionately to convince his audience of the continuing ministry of the Spirit among believers without being taken back by the fear of enthusiasm. Commenting on John 7:37–39, Whitefield notes that too many followers of Christ mistakenly believe that the spiritual experience of the first disciples was only meant for them rather than for Christians of all ages. It is the unfounded fear of being labeled an enthusiast—"madman," as he puts it—that fosters this highly reserved attitude toward the reception and ministry of the Spirit.[47]

Again, while resisting the temptation to make his hearers too excited about the more spectacular gifts of the Spirit,[48] Whitefield also urges all believers to open up their hearts for the manifold work of the Spirit:

> This blessed Spirit, who once moved on the face of the great deep; who overshadowed the blessed Virgin before that holy child was born of her; who

descended in a bodily shape, like a dove, on our blessed Lord, when he came up out of the water at his baptism; and afterwards came down in fiery tongues on the heads of all his Apostles at the day of Pentecost: this is the Holy Ghost, who must move on the faces of our souls; this power of the Most High, must come upon us, and we must be baptized with his baptism and refining fire, before we can be stiled true members of Christ's mystical body.[49]

The younger brother of John Wesley, Charles is most well known for his hymns. This short one was meant to be read before reading the Scripture:

Come, Holy Ghost, our hearts inspire,
Let us thine influence prove,
Source of the old prophetic fire,
Fountain of life and love.
Come, Holy Ghost (for moved by thee
The prophets wrote and spoke);
Unlock the truth, thyself the key,
Unseal the sacred book.
Expand thy wings, celestial dove,
Brood o'er our nature's night;
On our disordered spirits move,
And let there now be light.
God through himself we then shall know,
If thou within us shine;
And sound, with all thy saints below,
The depths of love divine.[50]

The Quakers

Officially known as the "Religious Society of Friends" or, for short, "Friends," the name "Quaker" was a nickname given by others because of spiritual manifestations such as shaking. In his highly acclaimed *Autobiography*, the founder George Fox gives us a vivid account of his deep and at times mystical religious experiences. Similarly to the mystics of the past, he had divine visitations, experienced a number of mighty spiritual experiences, and claimed to have spiritual gifts such as discernment. On one occasion he was filled with the love of God in a most remarkable way. By means of the "eternal light and power" he also saw what was done to Christ and how Christ conquers all powers of Satan.[51]

The formative spiritual experience for Fox—which also gave basic shape to Quakerism as a movement—was enlightenment with divine light:

Now the Lord God opened to me by His invisible power that every man was enlightened by the divine Light of Christ, and I saw it shine through all. . . . For I saw, in that Light and Spirit which was before the Scriptures were given forth, and which led the holy men of God to give them forth, that all, if they would know God or Christ, or the Scriptures aright, must come to that Spirit by which they that gave them forth were led and taught.[52]

A number of spiritual experiences followed in various locations.

Fox also claimed the exercise of spiritual discernment: "The Lord had given me a spirit of discerning, by which I many times saw the states and conditions of people, and could try their spirits," such as the state of possession by an evil spirit or hidden sexual sin.[53]

Whereas George Fox is the spiritual founder of the Friends, William Penn, the founder of Pennsylvania, was the visionary behind the sociopolitical freedom and liberty among the Friends. At the same time, Penn also helped defend and clarify the most well-known—and undoubtedly, most widely debated—idea of "light," the belief that within every believer God continues to speak (based on John 1:9). Penn claims that without "this principle of Light, Life, and Grace," there is no true conviction or conversion. A person without this light does not know sorrow for sin, nor experience new birth. It seems that for Penn the "Light" functions similarly to how the "Spirit" is conventionally known in the *ordo salutis*.[54] That this indeed is the case is confirmed by Penn himself. At times he equates the Holy Spirit with the "Light of God." The reasons he mentions for the equation include procession from God, the universal scope of presence and work, as well as works such as reproving and revelation.[55]

Jonathan Edwards and the Great Awakening

Considered by many to be one of the greatest preachers and churchmen in American history, Jonathan Edwards was instrumental also in the first Great Awakening. His theology displays a thick Spirit-Christology: "The sum of all that Christ purchased is the Holy Ghost. . . . The great thing purchased by Jesus Christ for us is communion with God, which is only in having the Spirit; 'tis participation of Christ's fullness, and having grace for grace, which is only in having of that Spirit which he has without measure."[56] In other words, everything Christ has to offer us comes from the Spirit. Edwards explains that the Spirit works in different ways in believers and nonbelievers. Whereas the Spirit exercises influence on both, in believers the Spirit dwells "as a vital principle," but in the unregenerate who do not possess the Spirit, the Spirit "operates only by assisting natural principles to do the same work which they do of themselves, to a greater degree." That is different from the "supernatural" work of the divine Spirit in those who have the Spirit.[57]

While Edwards was a profound evangelist calling for personal conversion, by no means was he oblivious to the communal aspects of the Spirit's work. Indeed, he surmises that an essential part of the Holy Spirit's role as "the holiness, or excellency and delight of God" has to do with the communion with God and communion with fellow men and women. To illustrate the communion among believers, Edwards employs familiar biblical metaphors, such as that of oil dripping from the high priest Aaron's head down to the skirts of his garments—a profound image of brotherly love in Psalm 133:

> The Spirit which Christ our Head has without measure is communicated to his church and people. The sweet perfumed oil signified Christ's excellency

and sweet delight [Philippians 2:1]. Communion, we know, is nothing else but the common partaking with others of good: communion with God is nothing else but a partaking with him of his excellency, his holiness and happiness.[58]

Like many great preachers and pastors, Edwards also considered carefully the issue of the "Sin against the Holy Ghost" in a sermon so titled. In his estimation, three things seem to be essential to this unpardonable sin, namely, "conviction, malice, and presumption (presumption in expressing that malice)." Only a person who knows something of the Holy Spirit can commit such sin. That person not only freely does evil works but also is presumptuous about his or her malice.[59]

THE SPIRIT IN NINETEENTH-CENTURY THEOLOGIES

The pneumatological contributions of the nineteenth-century theological movements come in three forms: modern Protestant theology (F. D. E. Schleiermacher and G. W. F. Hegel), the neo-Calvinist movement (e.g., A. Kuyper), and the so-called Reformed orthodoxy, closely allied with Princeton Seminary (B. B. Warfield, C. Hodge, and A. A. Hodge) and the Baptist A. H. Strong. These materials provide a transition to twentieth-century developments.

Friedrich D. E. Schleiermacher, appropriately named the "father of modern Protestant theology," deeply influenced by Pietism, Romanticism, and the philosophies of his time, produced a profound theology of the Spirit for the post-Enlightenment world. His contemporary Georg W. F. Hegel—perhaps the greatest philosopher since the masters of the ancient world such as Plato—brought about a world-embracing philosophical vision of the Spirit.

The neo-Calvinist school's views of the Spirit and salvation will be presented through the lens of its premier theologian, the Dutch Abraham Kuyper. Along with colleagues such as Herman Bavinck, Kuyper helped rediscover and upgrade the great Reformed traditions of pneumatology with a keen interest in sociopolitical and creational aspects along with salvation and Scripture.

Theologically more conservative, at times fundamentalist, Reformed pneumatology was developed and defended by the so-called Princeton orthodoxy, represented by three of its ablest theologians: B. B. Warfield and the two Hodges, Charles (father) and Archibald (son), as well as other like-minded theologians such as the Baptist Augustus Strong.

MODERN PROTESTANT THEOLOGY

Whereas the Enlightenment philosopher Immanuel Kant located religion in the realm of morality and the Idealist[60] philosopher G. W. F. Hegel in rational knowledge, for liberal theology the locus of religion and theology was to be found in "feeling"—a term not to be confused with the contemporary "thin" understanding of feeling as emotion but understood instead as a "thick" feeling of "absolute dependency," as Schleiermacher called it, a recognition of being referred to something "beyond."[61] In his masterful magnum opus *The Christian Faith* Schleiermacher proposes the basis for the Christian life as the union of the human with the divine Spirit, which also relates to his vision of the church as a community sharing the "common Spirit": "The Holy Spirit is the union of the Divine Essence with human nature in the form of the common Spirit animating the life in common of believers."[62] In other words, the Christian life is partaking of the Holy Spirit: "Every regenerate person partakes of the Holy Spirit, so that there is no living fellowship with Christ without an indwelling of the Holy Spirit, and vice versa."[63]

Schleiermacher's pneumatological soteriology is part of the discussion of the Christian community, the church. While the critics of the father of modern Protestant theology, particularly Karl Barth, were suspicious that for him the Holy Spirit was not divine but rather merely the "common [human or social] spirit," it is also true that Schleiermacher elevates the role of the Spirit in ecclesiology—and the relation of that to the indwelling of the Spirit in the believer—in a way that is yet to be fully appreciated.

> If now . . . we return to the point that in the Church from the beginning, and therefore already in the New Testament, all the powers at work in the Christian Church—and not merely the miraculous gifts, which in this connexion are quite accidental—are traced to the Holy Spirit; and if we ask what is thus supposed to have been present from the very start, the following admissions have to be made. . . . These powers are not to be found outside of the Christian Church, and hence they neither arise from the general constitution of human nature . . . nor from any other divine arrangement. . . . [Furthermore], the Holy Spirit is not something that, although divine, is not united with the human nature, but only somehow influences it from without. For whatever enters us from without does so only through the senses and never becomes more than an occasion for our action. What action is to follow on this occasion is determined from within, and only this, and not the former region of the senses, is the sphere of the Holy Spirit. . . . There is indeed no way of imagining how the Spirit's gifts could be within us, and He Himself remain without. . . .[64]

Examining in the same context two thinkers as diverse as Schleiermacher and Hegel may give rise to the misunderstanding that these two share materially similar kinds of views. The only reason these two giants are treated together is that they stand between the Reformation and the twentieth century as representatives of the best of the Enlightenment heritage in their passion to revise the Christian understanding of reality and theology. In his *Early Theological Writings*, Hegel is drawn to the mystical milieu of the Gospel of John. Considering the union of the divine and human in Jesus' incarnation, Hegel speaks of faith as the "relation of spirit to spirit": "Spirit alone recognizes spirit." The Jews failed to see in Jesus who he really was because "the essence of Jesus, i.e., his relationship to God as son to father, can be truly grasped only by faith. . . . How could anything but a spirit know a spirit?"[65]

In his most famous work, *The Phenomenology of the Spirit*, Hegel sets forth his speculative theory of incarnation, which of course resembles the classical Christian idea but also goes far beyond it. The same can be said of his profound vision of the Trinity and the role of the Spirit therein. His work *Lectures on the Philosophy of Religions* brings to culmination his Trinitarian vision as part of his reflections on religion. In the Godhead, there are three moments of divine reality, something similar to the Christian doctrine of the Trinity. "Eternal" or "Essential Being," "the idea of God of and in itself," is something similar to the Father or immanent Trinity; "representation" or "the form of appearance, that of particularization, of being for others" echoes the Christian idea of the incarnate Son; and finally, the "form of return from appearance to itself" or "absolute self-consciousness" or "absolute presence-to-self" resembles the Holy Spirit, which manifests itself in community and cult. Thus in Hegel's world-embracing system the final goal of all historical happening and the process of the Spirit is God's returning to himself in humanity. This takes place in the religious life in which humanity comes to know God as God knows himself. This is the final reconciliation within reality.[66] Related to the "third element" in the Trinitarian movement of the Spirit is the emergence of the community. As is well known, Hegel believed that it is in Protestant communities that the "turn to inwardness" is best expressed, compared to Catholicism, which in his estimation was more "external" and "objectifying."[67] Indeed, Hegel calls this transition from externality to internality the "outpouring of the Spirit."[68]

In sum, both Schleiermacher and Hegel, in their own respective ways, sought to rediscover and reinterpret pneumatology in terms of current philosophical, cultural, and theological developments. In contrast, with an at times abstract and revisionist approach, the neo-Calvinist school sought to stand on the shoulders of reformed Reformers and build on the classical biblical and theological tradition to make the talk about the Spirit more meaningful for the people of the nineteenth century.

The Neo-Calvinist School

A Dutch Christian minister and theologian who toward the end of his productive life was appointed prime minister of the Netherlands in the beginning of the twentieth century, Abraham Kuyper was also a journalist, founder of the Anti-Revolutionary party, and a key player in the founding of the Free University of Amsterdam. In his main pneumatological work *The Work of the Holy Spirit*—in the long line of the Reformed tradition—Kuyper presents a fairly typical *ordo salutis*, order of salvation, in which he presents the typical stages of the Reformed understanding of the order of salvation as the works of the Holy Spirit.[69]

One of Kuyper's greatest contributions was the development of the Reformed idea of "common grace" pneumatologically conceived:

Naturally . . . we have to distinguish between the two very distinct operations of common grace. Though "common grace" impacts the whole of our human life, it does not impact all aspects of this life in the same way. One common grace aims at the *interior*, another at the *exterior* part of our existence. The former is operative wherever civic virtue, a sense of domesticity, natural love, the practice of human virtue, the improvement of the public conscience, integrity, mutual loyalty among people, and a feeling for piety leaven life. The latter is in evidence when human power over nature increases, when invention upon invention enriches life, when international communication is improved, the arts flourish, the sciences increase our understanding, the conveniences and joys of life multiply, all expressions of life become more vital and radiant, forms become more refined, and the general image of life becomes more winsome. . . .[70]

Common grace, says Kuyper, "opens a history, unlocks an enormous space of time, triggers a vast and long-lasting string of events, . . . precipitates a series of successive generations . . . [so that] every century teaches us that new things added each time surpass all that has been imagined before."[71] While distinctions should be made for the sake of theological clarity, the Dutch theologian also emphasizes that there is but one grace of God when it comes to the work of the Spirit.[72] Typical of Kuyper, his exposition of the work of grace with regard to salvation is inclusive and challenges a typical misunderstanding according to which grace would merely help the sinner return, as it were, to the original state of blessedness. The Spirit works both in the realm of grace and the realm of nature, thus encompassing the whole activity of God in the world and salvation. Thus, when God justifies the person he is not only returning the original righteousness but also renewing the person so that the person may do the works of new life.[73]

While Kuyper's main pneumatological work, *The Work of the Holy Spirit*, focuses on soteriological aspects of the Spirit's work, it is by no means limited to these aspects. The Spirit's work also embraces the natural order:

From the whole Scripture teaching we therefore conclude that the Holy Spirit has a work in connection with mechanical arts and official functions—in every special talent whereby some men excel in such art or office. This teaching is not simply that such gifts and talents are not of man but from God like all other blessings, but that they are not the work of the Father, nor of the son, but of the Holy Spirit.[74]

Yet another indication of Kuyper's inclusive—at times quite bold—approach is his extended discussion of speaking in tongues. It is a topic most Reformed scholars, both of old and his contemporaries, avoided because of the idea of cessationism, according to which spiritual gifts had ceased once the canon of the Bible was ratified. Kuyper considers carefully the signs following the outpouring of the Spirit and concludes, "Hence on Pentecost there was the miracle of tongues in its perfection; later on in the churches, in weaker measure."[75]

Herman Bavinck, Kuyper's successor as professor of theology at the Free University of Amsterdam, continued developing a profound and inclusive pneumatology. The newly translated fourth volume of his four-volume *Reformed Dogmatics*, titled *Holy Spirit, Church, and New Creation*, constructs soteriology, ecclesiology, and eschatology in a pneumatological perspective. The main headings of the three-part work indicate Bavinck's approach: "The Spirit Gives New Life to Believers"; "The Spirit Creates New Community"; and "The Spirit Makes All Things New." In the ecclesiology section, headings such as "The Church's Spiritual Essence" (chap. 5), "The Church's Spiritual Government" (chap. 6), and "The Church's Spiritual Power" (chap. 8) well illustrate the thoroughgoing pneumatological undergirding of his theology.[76]

The Reformed Orthodoxy

The common denominator between the neo-Calvinist school and Princeton orthodoxy is an attempt by Reformed theologians to rediscover the meaning and significance of biblical and historical Christian faith vis-à-vis current challenges. The difference has to do with theological orientation: while the former placed itself within mainline Protestant theology, the Princeton theologians, as well as like-minded scholars such as A. H. Strong, advocated a highly conservative, virtually fundamentalist agenda.

For half a century, the three-volume *Systematic Theology* by Charles Hodge, professor of theology at Princeton Seminary, was a standard conservative doctrinal manual. An important concern for Hodge was the defense of the divine inspiration of Scripture and the Spirit's role therein. However, while staunchly arguing for divine inspiration, Hodge found it crucial to reject any notion of a mechanical "dictation" theory of inspiration.[77] Hodge's colleague at Princeton, Benjamin Breckinridge Warfield, coauthored an essay titled "The Authority and Inspiration of the Scripture" that became a magna carta of conservative Christianity for many generations. While not putting aside the human element, Warfield explains that the meaning of divine inspiration is that "it puts behind the human also a divine authorship. It ascribes to the authors such an attending influence of the Spirit in the process of writing, that the words they set down become also the words of God."[78]

In keeping with tradition, the Princeton theologians also offered a wide discussion of the relationship between grace and the Spirit. Following Calvin, Hodge argues that an "inward teaching by the Spirit is absolutely necessary to give the truth effect. This distinction between the outward teaching of the Word and the inward teaching of the Spirit is kept up throughout the Scriptures."[79] Hodge's soteriological work *The Way of Life* uses traditional Reformed terminology and approaches to expand the discussion of the role of the Spirit in salvation.[80]

The son of Charles Hodge, Archibald, the principal of Princeton, penned his *Outlines of Theology* in a way that made it a milestone defense of conservative Christian doctrines. Filled with scriptural references and highly nuanced argumentation—in the best tradition of Protestant scholasticism—A. A. Hodge clarifies the nature of the Holy Spirit by responding to questions such as the following:

> 31. How can it be proved that all the attributes of personality are ascribed to the Holy Ghost in the Scriptures? . . .
>
> 34. How may his personality be proved by what is said of the sin against the Holy Ghost? . . .
>
> 35. How can such expressions as "giving" and "pouring out the Spirit" be reconciled with his personality? . . .
>
> 40. How can such expressions as, "he shall not speak of himself" be reconciled with his divinity?[81]

One of Warfield's more polemical writings is titled *Counterfeit Miracles,* in which he vehemently defends the idea of cessationism, the belief that miracles ceased after the closing of the canon in the fourth century because external "proofs" were no longer needed alongside Scripture. Similarly in his essay "The Cessation of the Charismata," he surmises that, on the one hand, we should not undermine but rather give full credit to the plethora of miracles accompanying the ministry of Jesus. Indeed, they were so many that the Lord "banished disease and death from Palestine for the three years of His ministry." On the other hand, Warfield surmises that the miraculous activity was the "characterizing peculiarity of specifically the Apostolic Church, and it belonged therefore exclusively to the Apostolic age." The miraculous gifts were "distinctively the authentication of the Apostles," part of the "credentials of the Apostles as the authoritative agents of God in founding the church." They were confined to the apostolic era and have ceased thereafter.[82] The cessationist argument, of course, became a major tool against the rising pentecostal and charismatic movements. Strangely enough, while the conservative-fundamentalist and pentecostal/charismatic movements shared a number of key theological beliefs in their affirmation of classical Christianity, the cessationist argument caused deep divisions and suspicion between the two movements.

Sharp thinkers and apologists, the Princeton theologians also knew the importance of a pastoral approach to doctrine and spirituality. In his semipopular writing *The Power of God unto Salvation,* Warfield offers a fascinating discussion of the ancient idea of the Holy Spirit as love:

> The Father is no more love, and the Son is no more love, than the Spirit is love; and when we confess that God is love, we confess by necessary implication that the Holy Spirit, who is God, is Himself love. But it will be far more to the point for us to ask ourselves in all seriousness if we have been in the habit of realizing to ourselves the blessed fact that the Holy Spirit loves us. This does not seem to be a form of gratulation in which Christians are accustomed to felicitate themselves.[83]

Chapter 6

The Spirit
in Twentieth-Century
Interpretations

Not surprisingly, the pneumatologies of the twentieth century and the beginning of the third millennium reflect the diversity and plurality characteristic of all contemporary theologies. In addition to diversity, there is also an unprecedented pneumatological interest, perhaps even an enthusiasm. The rich flow of academic publications alongside various scholarly events devoted to the Holy Spirit are but the tip of the iceberg in the current pneumatological renaissance. There is also a widespread hunger for the Holy Spirit and spiritual experiences among Christian churches and believers.

While pneumatological and soteriological traditions are being revisited, reinterpreted, and reconfigured as an essential part of the continuing constructive work, a new breed of pneumatological interpretations is also emerging, including feminist and other women's interpretations, liberationist, sociopolitical, and ecological pneumatologies. True, none of these themes is absolutely new and untried in Christian theology; think only of the diversity of themes in medieval interpretations of the Spirit. Yet in a real sense there is much that is new in the intensity, breadth, and depth of these so-called contextual views.

This section will first present and discuss the main theologico-ecclesiastical traditions in pneumatology—from the newest group, the pentecostal/charismatic movements, to the oldest church, the Eastern Orthodox Church. Both denominational views and theologies of leading individual theologians will be discussed. The last part of this section will probe contextual interpretations, including the views of women and other liberationists as well those with political and ecological perspectives and concerns.

PENTECOSTAL AND CHARISMATIC MOVEMENTS

A fitting way to open up the discussion of the Holy Spirit in twentieth-century theology and spirituality is to highlight the significance and contribution of the set of movements whose origin can be found at the turn of that century and whose growth has been phenomenal, namely, the pentecostal and charismatic movements. It is useful to follow the typology suggested by *The New International Dictionary of Pentecostal and Charismatic Movements*:[1] first, classical pentecostal denominations, such as Assemblies of God or Foursquare Gospel, that owe their existence to the famous Azusa revival; second, charismatic movements and pentecostal-type spiritual movements within the established churches (the largest of which is the Roman Catholic charismatic renewal); and third, neocharismatic movements, some of the most notable of which are the Vineyard Fellowship in the U.S.A., African Initiated Churches, and the China House Church movement, as well as an innumerable number of independent churches and groups all over the world. In terms of participation, the charismatic movements (about 200 million) and neocharismatics (200–300 million) well outnumber classical Pentecostals (75–125 million).

Because of the overwhelming diversity of the movement—internationally, culturally, and with regard to "ethos"—the determination of common features of pneumatology is an extremely challenging task.[2] If there is a common denominator, not only among classical Pentecostals but also between them and, say, Roman Catholic charismatics and African instituted churches, it has to do with a unique spirituality. While it can be identified in more than one way, it has everything to do with a Christ-centered charismatic spirituality characterized by a passionate desire to "meet" with Jesus Christ, who is perceived as the bearer of the "full gospel," that is, Jesus as savior, sanctifier, healer, baptizer with the Spirit, and the soon-returning king.[3] Another way of speaking of the pentecostal view of the Spirit is to refer to the category of "empowerment," which Harvard theologian Harvey Cox names "primal spirituality." For Cox, the Harvard University observer of global Pentecostalism, that movement represents a spiritual restoration of significance and purpose to lift people from despair and hopelessness.[4] Whereas for most other Christians the presence of the Spirit is just that, *presence,* for Pentecostals the presence of the Spirit in their midst implies *empowerment.* While this empowerment often manifests itself in spiritual gifts such as speaking in tongues, prophesy, or healings, it is still felt and sought by Pentecostals even when those manifestations are absent. Pentecostalism has thus offered a grassroots challenge to established churches and theologies, especially those endorsing the so-called cessationist principle, which holds that miracles or extraordinary charismata ceased at or near the end of the apostolic age.[5] Often ridiculed for emotionalism, Pentecostals introduced a dynamic, enthusiastic type of spirituality and worship life to the contemporary church, emphasizing the possibility of experiencing God mystically. Pentecostals call this initial empowerment experience Spirit baptism.[6]

While the experience rather than the doctrine came first, a novel and disputed doctrinal understanding of Spirit baptism emerged in the early years of the movement.[7] While never uniformly formulated nor followed by the worldwide movement, it is only fair to say that for the large majority of Pentecostals, this view came to be known as the "initial physical evidence." This simply means that Pentecostals expect an external sign or marker of the reception of Spirit baptism, namely, speaking in tongues (glossolalia). Pentecostals claim this doctrine comes from the book of Acts, their favorite book, and from contemporary experience.[8] Other gifts of the Spirit, such as prophesying, prayer for healing, and works of miracles, are enthusiastically embraced and sought by Pentecostals. A related belief is the capacity to fight "spiritual warfare" and exorcise demonic spirits, if necessary. This belief is a significant part of pentecostal spirituality, especially outside the West.[9]

The belief in the capacity of the Spirit to bring about healing, whether physical or mental, is one of the hallmarks of Pentecostalism. According to the leading pentecostal theologian Amos Yong, at the heart of pentecostal pneumatology is a holistic view of salvation that is

> in contrast to soteriologies that tend to bifurcate the work of Christ and of the Spirit, such as those articulated by Protestant scholasticism. In that framework, Christ provides salvation objectively (e.g., in justification) and the Spirit accomplishes salvation subjectively (e.g., in sanctification). In response, a [pentecostal] pneumatological soteriology understands salvation to be the work of both Christ and the Spirit from beginning to end. . . . In all of this, the Spirit is not an appendage to Christ in the process of salvation but saves with Christ throughout.[10]

The holistic orientation has intensified and become more holistic in recent years as Pentecostals in Latin America and elsewhere become stronger in their sociopolitical concerns. According to Yong, "such engagement shows an emerging awareness that salvation is not only an otherworldly anticipation but also a this-worldly experience, manifest in the material, economic, social, and political dimensions of human existence."[11]

Two interrelated features need to be added to aptly characterize the distinctive features of the pentecostal view of the Spirit: eschatology and missionary enthusiasm. From the beginning, Pentecostals were convinced that the twentieth-century outpouring of the Spirit marked the beginning of the return of Jesus Christ to establish the kingdom. In the meantime, based on biblical promises such as Acts

1:8, Christians were supposed to be empowered by the Spirit to bring the gospel to all nations. As a result of this "eschatological urgency,"[12] a massive missionary and evangelistic enterprise emerged, a main factor in the continuing rapid growth of the movement.

Yong summarizes succinctly the nature of pentecostal pneumatology and also points to its relation to other pneumatologies:

> In Pentecostalism, as in most conservative, traditionalist, and evangelical Christian traditions, the orthodox doctrine of the Holy Spirit as divine person continues to prevail. Yet Pentecostals go beyond many of their orthodox Christian kindred to say that the Holy Spirit continues to act in the world and interact personally with human beings and communities. In this tradition, then, there is the ongoing expectation of the Holy Spirit's answer to intercessory prayer, of the Spirit's continual and personal intervention in the affairs of the world and in the lives of believers even when not specifically prayed for, and of the Spirit's manifestation in the charismatic or spiritual gifts (as enumerated by St. Paul in 1 Corinthians 12:4–7). Of course, amidst all that occurs in Pentecostal circles are some rather fantastic accounts . . . and discerning between the valid and the spurious is not always easy. Pentecostals face the tension of (on the one hand) accepting a rather traditional supernaturalistic worldview along with at least some of the more embarrassing claims that come with it, resulting in their being excluded from scholarly or academic conversation, or (on the other hand) attempting to reinterpret Pentecostal testimonies within a more naturalistic framework so as to be able to proceed acceptably with rigorous scientific inquiry into Pentecostal spirituality and experience.[13]

EASTERN ORTHODOX SPIRITUALITY

Discussing the pneumatology and spirituality of the contemporary Eastern Orthodox Church following that of Pentecostalism means a transition from the newest to the oldest tradition! Essential to any statement on contemporary doctrine of the Spirit among the Eastern churches is the acknowledgment of the primacy of tradition. The core teaching about the Holy Spirit in the Christian East, even in the beginning of the twenty-first century, is the sacred tradition of the church fathers and subsequent saints of the church.

> Just as the Grace of the Holy Spirit which descended on the Apostles at Pentecost flows in a living stream down through today's bishops and priests, so Sacred Tradition carries the spiritual life of the Church in an unbroken stream from the time of the Apostles down to Orthodox believers today. . . . The power of Sacred Tradition is the power of the Holy Spirit as it influences Orthodox Christians in all ages.[14]

In keeping with tradition, Eastern Orthodox theology approaches the Spirit— as any other topic of faith—from a mystical, prayerful, and apophatic perspective rather than a primarily discursive, analytic, and "academic" one. The title of

Vladimir Lossky's important work *The Mystical Theology of the Eastern Orthodox Church*, reveals this orientation. Another case in point is the eulogy given by Metropolitan Evloghios on the occasion of the passing away of Sergius Bulgakov, a leading former-generation mystical theologian whose work *Comforter* has become a classic in pneumatology and spirituality.[15] The eulogy said the following of this saint:

> You were enlightened by the Holy Spirit, the Spirit of Wisdom, the Spirit of Understanding, the Comforter to Whom you dedicated your scholarly work. . . . He guided you to your last breath. Twenty-six years ago you partook of His gracious gifts in the sacrament of ordination and you bore the cross of priesthood in the Holy Spirit. It is significant that you received this gift on the day of the Holy Spirit—when He descended upon the holy apostles in tongues of fire. Thus you had a share in them. . . . It is significant too that you celebrated your last liturgy on earth on that very day of the Holy Spirit, the anniversary of your ordination as a priest.[16]

Due to the continuing resistance to the filioque clause because of its subordination of the Spirit to the Son, Eastern Orthodox theologians continue to speak about the work of the Spirit and Son as parallel to each other.[17] Again, in line with tradition, Eastern theologians continue speaking of the Spirit's role in salvation in term of *theosis*, deification.[18] Lossky explains the coming of the Holy Spirit to deify human beings and the Spirit's own "shy" nature:

> The Holy Spirit communicates Himself *to persons*, marking each member of the Church with a seal of personal and unique relationship to the Trinity, becoming present in each person. How does this come about? That remains a mystery—the mystery of the self-emptying, of the *kenosis* of the Holy Spirit's coming into the world. If in the *kenosis* of the Son the Person appeared to men while the Godhead remained hidden under the form of a servant, the Holy Spirit in His coming, while He manifests the common nature of the Trinity, leaves His own Person concealed beneath His Godhead. He remains unrevealed, hidden, so to speak, by the gift in order that this gift which He imparts may be fully ours, adapted to our persons.[19]

While deification is a personal experience, the church is the "sphere within which union with God takes place in this present life," and therefore "the Church surpasses the earthly paradise." That is because "in the Church and through the sacraments our nature enters into union with the divine nature in the hypostasis of the Son, the Head of His mystical body. Our humanity becomes consubstantial with the deified humanity, united with the person of Christ."[20]

Understandably, therefore, the doctrine of the church in the Christian East is more pneumatologically loaded than ecclesiologies of the Christian West.[21] This is most forcefully brought home by the famous claim of John Zizioulas's communion theology—after the title of his work *Being as Communion*—according to which communion and relationship belong to the very essence of *personal* being, as in the community of the three divine persons. The role of the Spirit, the Spirit of *koinōnia*, is to create and sustain this communion:

> It is not enough to speak of eschatology and communion as necessary aspects of Pneumatology and ecclesiology; it is necessary to make these aspects of Pneumatology *constitutive* of ecclesiology. What I mean by "constitutive" is that these aspects of Pneumatology must qualify the very ontology of the Church. The Spirit is not something that "animates" a Church which already somehow exists. The Spirit makes the Church *be*. Pneumatology does not refer to the well-being but to the very being of the Church. It is not about a dynamism which is added to the essence of the Church. It is the very essence of the Church. The Church is *constituted* in and through eschatology and communion. Pneumatology is an ontological category in ecclesiology. . . .[22]

The Eastern Orthodox tradition is known for its cosmic orientation. In the doctrine of the church it comes to the fore in the idea of the church as a "microcosm" of the universe or in theological anthropology with its view of the human person as a cosmos in miniature. In the doctrine of creation, a robust view of the Spirit in the world, all over the created cosmos, emerges, as is evident in the work of the Rumanian Dumitru Staniloae. One of the ways that Staniloae—whose many writings have been translated into English only recently—illustrates the cosmic domain of the Spirit is in the Spirit's capacity both to intervene in the happenings of the world, including all processes of nature, and to "render the effects of these interventions much more extensive, more sensible, and more efficacious than the interventions of human freedom."[23] Significantly enough, the late Rumanian theologian also develops a robust pneumatological account of theological anthropology.[24]

ROMAN CATHOLIC PNEUMATOLOGIES

More than any other church, the Roman Catholic Church has attempted to define its doctrine and spirituality by means of official documents. Several popes during the past century have issued significant encyclicals on pneumatology, such as *Divinum illud munus* (On the Holy Spirit) by Pope Leo in 1897 and *Mystici Corporis Christi* (On the Mystical Body of Christ) by Pope Pius XII in 1943. Pius made a significant contribution to the rediscovery of the role of the Spirit in ecclesiology and spiritual life. A highly significant Catholic teaching on the Holy Spirit was provided by the late John Paul II in his *Dominum et vivificantem* (On the Holy Spirit in the Life of the Church and the World) in 1986.[25] Going beyond the animating role given to the Holy Spirit by his predecessor, John Paul II's edict taught that

> between the Holy Spirit and Christ there thus subsists, in the economy of salvation, an intimate bond, whereby the Spirit works in human history as "another Counselor". . . . Thus, in the Holy Spirit-Paraclete, who in the mystery and action of the Church unceasingly continues the historical presence on earth of the Redeemer and his saving work, the glory of Christ shines forth." (# 7)

The late pope also spoke strongly about the Spirit's role in bringing salvation to men and women—which means nothing less than drawing humanity into the Trinitarian union with Father, Son, and Spirit (# 39, 65).

The decisive turn in Roman Catholic theology in general and in pneumatology in particular came with the Second Vatican Council (1962–65).[26] Pope John XXIII, when formally announcing the council, wrote, "This getting together of all the bishops of the Church should be like a new Pentecost." This council could be called the "Council of the Holy Spirit," for as Pope Paul VI pointed out, the pages of the council documents contain two hundred and fifty-eight references to the Holy Spirit.[27] The Spirit's role in Scripture and revelation is discussed in one of the most important Vatican II documents, *Dei Verbum* (*Dogmatic Constitution on Divine Revelation*), which presents the contemporary Catholic theology of revelation.[28] The Holy Spirit's aid is needed in the assent to the divine truth revealed to human beings in Christ (#5). Undoubtedly, the most important Vatican II document is *Lumen Gentium* (*Dogmatic Constitution on the Church*), the statement on the doctrine of the church. In a Trinitarian framework, the Spirit who with Christ gathers together the faithful from all nations, helps unceasingly renew Christians (#7). In a remarkable way, the document speaks of the "entire body of the faithful, anointed as they are by the Holy One, [which] cannot err in matters of belief" because of the "supernatural discernment in matters of faith." This people of God is sanctified and led not only by means of the sacraments and the ministries but also through the allotment of "gifts to everyone according as He wills. . . . By these gifts He makes them fit and ready to undertake the various tasks and offices which contribute toward the renewal and building up of the Church" (#12). In keeping with the current understanding, Vatican II defined the church as mission, rather than mission being merely a task assigned to the church. In the missionary life and activity, the Spirit is the guide and source of power as explained in the missionary document, *Ad Gentes* (*Degree on the Mission Activity of the Church*) (#2).

One of the key concerns behind the convening of the Second Vatican Council was the need to respond to the challenges and needs of contemporary times. *Gaudium et Spes* (*Pastoral Constitution on the Church in the Modern World*) is the document that tackles issues of secularism, atheism, technology, politics, and the like. Its approach is decidedly pneumatological, for it sees the whole of humanity being united because of a common origin and destiny. In keeping with the contemporary Catholic theology of religions, according to which salvation in Christ through the Spirit is also available to people who have never heard the gospel (should they follow the light given in their own religion and pursue moral guidelines), the document makes a profound statement on the Spirit's role in making salvation available to people in other faiths. Having explained all the great blessings of the faithful, such as love, assurance of spiritual inheritance, and the hope for resurrection, *Gaudium et Spes* states,

All this holds true not only for Christians, but for all men of good will in whose hearts grace works in an unseen way. For, since Christ died for all men, and since the ultimate vocation of man is in fact one, and divine, we ought to believe that the Holy Spirit in a manner known only to God offers to every man the possibility of being associated with this paschal mystery. (#22)

Several theologians played a crucial role in initiating a fuller recovery of the doctrine of the Holy Spirit on the eve of Vatican II and afterwards, such as the Swiss Hans Urs von Balthasar, the French Yves Marie Joseph Congar,[29] and the Austrian Karl Rahner.[30] The "theologian of beauty," von Balthasar devotes the last part of his celebrated trilogy *The Glory of the Lord*, *Theo-Drama*, and *Theo-Logic* to a volume titled *The Spirit of Truth*. In keeping with tradition stemming from St. Augustine, the Swiss theologian suggests a number of names to highlight the manifold ministry of the Spirit, such as gift (Rom. 5:5), freedom (2 Cor. 3:17), and inward and outward testimony (John 15:26).[31] A rare combination of profound intellect and mystical spirituality, Balthasar's meditation *The Conquest of the Bride* builds on long Catholic spiritual tradition and Bible exposition. In this devotional, he also speaks of the unity the Spirit brings to the church.[32]

The French Dominican Congar's three-volume *I Believe in the Holy Spirit* has already established itself as a contemporary classic. Always keen on tradition, Congar speaks widely about the dynamic and charismatic nature of the spiritual life in the early centuries of the church: "The apostles set out, filled with the assurance of the Holy Spirit, to proclaim the good news of the coming of the kingdom of heaven. In the beginning, the Church saw itself as subject to the activity of the Spirit and filled with his gifts." He mentions that at this time there was not yet a clash between "charism" and "institution" nor between "gifting" and "ministry."[33] A great champion of the renewal of the Catholic Church, Congar made every effort to draw from the rich resources of *Lumen Gentium*, particularly with regard to a renewed spiritual and charismatic life. He also gave full support to the work of the charismatic renewal in his church.[34] Among such typical topics as the inspiration of Scripture, soteriology, and the church, Congar also inquires into theological anthropology through the lens of pneumatology. In keeping with a holistic Catholic approach, the French theologian speaks of all aspects of the human being's life, whether ordinary everyday or "spiritual" life, as the domain of the Holy Spirit.[35]

The name of the German-Austrian Jesuit Karl Rahner towers highest among the Catholic thinkers of the last decades of the second millennium. Contrary to older scholastic theology "from above," Rahner's approach set out to develop a genuinely Christian theology "from below," from the concrete historical particularity of human existence and the coming-to-humanity in the incarnation of the triune God. He believed that "God . . . has already communicated himself in his Holy Spirit always and everywhere and to every person as the innermost center of his existence."[36] This is possible because the human being has been created in a way that he can participate in God's being.[37] It is a profound anthropological statement indeed! He himself draws the obvious conclusion that grace is nothing less than God's self-giving. Differently from scholastic theology in which grace was "created" and thus could not be identified with God himself, for Rahner grace is "uncreated" because God gave himself in the person of the Holy Spirit:

> If God as he is in himself has already communicated himself in his Holy Spirit always and everywhere and to every person as the innermost center of his [the individual person's] existence, whether he wants it or not, whether he reflects upon it or not, whether he accepts it or not, and if the whole history of creation is already borne by God's self-communication in this very creation, then there does not seem to be anything else which can take place on God's part.[38]

Similarly to his French colleague, this Austrian theologian was also deeply concerned about the renewal of the church. In a passionate appeal, "Do Not Stifle the Spirit," he called the church not to be bound to ecclesiastical authority and structures in a way that could make her deaf to the invitations of the Spirit.[39] Right at the time when Vatican Council II was in session, he published another appeal for the charismata in the church, titled *The Dynamic Element in the Church*. Rahner suggested that one must learn to perceive charismata when they first appear, rather than canonize charismatic persons after their death.[40]

Among the living Roman Catholic pneumatologists, few have exercised more influence and published more widely on various aspects of the doctrine of the Spirit, both historical and contemporary, than the American Benedictine Fr. Kilian McDonnell. Earlier in his career, he also published widely on the Roman Catholic charismatic renewal, and he has been instrumental in the international dialogue between the Vatican and Pentecostals. Fr. Kilian laments the limited, secondary role given to the Holy Spirit both in Catholic and Protestant theology:

> In both Protestantism and Catholicism, the doctrine of the Holy Spirit, or pneumatology, has to do mostly with private, not public experience. In Protestantism, the interest in pneumatology has been largely in pietism where it is a function of interiority and inwardness. In Roman Catholicism, its dominant expression has been in books on spirituality or on the charismatic renewal, or when speaking of the structural elements of the church. In the West, we think essentially in Christological categories, with the Holy Spirit as an extra, an addendum, a "false" window to give symmetry and balance to theological design. We build up our large theological constructs in constitutive Christological categories, and then, in a second, nonconstitutive moment, we decorate the already constructed system with pneumatological baubles, a little Spirit tinsel.[41]

With many contemporaries, the Benedictine theologian is searching for a more inclusive, life-affirming approach to the Spirit because "contemporary theology has turned from a theology of the Word to a theology of the World."[42] Thus he titled his recently released landmark work *The Other Hand of God: The Holy*

Spirit as the Universal Touch and Goal, a work that has established his place among leading Catholic theologians of the Spirit.

As a theologian and a monk, McDonnell always emphasizes the integral relation of theology to spirituality and liturgy. He reminds us that past great works on the Spirit and the Trinity, such as Basil's *On the Holy Spirit* and Richard's *On the Trinity*, were born in the midst of liturgical and doxological settings. As a theologian and a poet, he also asks, Would it be possible to construct a contemporary Trinitarian and pneumatological theology that without losing philosophical acumen and anchoring in tradition, could also manifest poetic "aesthetic, hymnodic, and doxological images, so that one can pray and preach and celebrate it? Doxology alone speaks the language of this contemplative country."[43] Another important "turn" suggested by this Benedictine theologian is suggested in the title of his chapter "To Do Pneumatology Is to Do Eschatology." There he argues that in the biblical account the Spirit of God appears both in the beginning and the end of the Story, God's story.[44]

PROTESTANT THEOLOGIES OF THE HOLY SPIRIT

Unlike Eastern Orthodox and Roman Catholic theologians, leading Protestant theologians, while they often glean from the resources of their own traditions, are not necessarily limited by nor are they always faithful representatives of their particular church context. This discussion is broken into three sections. The first section briefly considers various approaches to the Spirit in the mid-twentieth-century Protestant theologies as modalistic, liberal, and neoorthodox proposals debate one another. The second section, the largest one, focuses on three Reformed theologians and one Lutheran theologian, all living, who have outlined profound pneumatological programs. The third section consists of the emerging pneumatologies from the "evangelical" movements.

Pneumatological "Turns"

The Dutch Hendrikus Berkhof attempted a powerful revision of traditional confessional Reformed theology in light of the heritage of classical liberalism and the new challenges of the twentieth-century context. In his 1964 *The Doctrine of the Holy Spirit*, Berkhof put forth a strongly modalistically oriented pneumatology in which the Spirit is hardly more than an efficacy of God. The Spirit simply means the "vitality" of God, "God's inspiring breath by which he grants life in creation and re-creation."[45] The role of the Spirit as the giver of life comes to the fore in regeneration, Berkhof's favored term for salvation.[46] While strongly modalistic, Berkhof's view of the Spirit is also inclusive and universalistic. On the one hand, it builds on the Reformed tradition stemming from Calvin and Kuyper and, on the other, it anticipates the contemporary turn to a holistic doctrine of the Spirit. In other words, we discern God's acts through the Spirit in history, in creation and preservation, as well as in human life. Echoing Kuyper, Berkhof concludes that "the Spirit of God also inspires man's culture. The Old Testament connects him with agriculture, architecture, jurisdiction, and politics (Cyrus as God's anointed one!). In general all human wisdom is the gift of God's Spirit. This relation between the Spirit and creation is much neglected in Christian thinking";[47] furthermore "the Spirit is not locked up in the church."[48] Another strongly modalistically oriented pneumatological program, which also drinks from liberal wells, is that of the Anglican Geoffrey Lampe. In his *God as Spirit* Lampe seeks to set aside the metaphysical questions, for the Spirit of which he is speaking, in line with Schleiermacher, is the personal presence of God, first and foremost in Christ and then in his followers:

> We are speaking of God disclosed and experienced as Spirit: that is, in his personal outreach. The use of this concept allows us to say that God indwelt and motivated the human spirit of Jesus in such a way that in him, uniquely, the relationship for which man was intended by his Creator was fully realized; that through Jesus God acted decisively to cause men to share in his relationship to God, and that the same God, the Spirit who was in Jesus, brings believers into that relationship of "sonship" towards himself and forms them into a human community in which, albeit partially and imperfectly, the Christlike character which is the fruit of their relationship is re-presented.[49]

A powerful rebuttal of Berkhof's and Lampe's approaches was offered by the "church father of the twentieth century," the Swiss Reformed theologian Karl Barth. In reaction to his own liberal training, Barth developed a theology that was fully Trinitarian and totally opposed to anything liberal. Barth's theology in general and pneumatology in particular are characterized by an uncompromising dialectic between the divine and human, in complete rejection of liberalism's continuity principle: "The Spirit guarantees man what he cannot guarantee himself, his personal participation in revelation."[50] Another key concern for Barth was the maintenance of the full, absolute freedom of the triune God. The Holy Spirit is the one who establishes and guarantees freedom, he surmises, taking his lead from the biblical affirmation "Where the Spirit of the Lord is, there is freedom" (2 Cor. 3:17).[51] Importantly, Barth begins his massive multivolume *Church Dogmatics* with the Trinity. Trinitarian doctrine, rather than being based on speculation, is based on the biblical view of revelation: "God reveals himself. He reveals himself through himself. He reveals himself."[52] While different from Berkhof, ironically Barth was suspected of a modalistic orientation in his theology because of his reluctance to apply the concept of "person" to Trinitarian members because of its alleged individualistic connotations in modern theology. Instead, he uses the term "modes of being" (from German *Seinsweise*, which, however does not denote "modalism" as does the English). Barth names the Spirit "Revealedness," along with the Father as the Revealer and the Son as Revelation.[53] It is in this Revealedness, "in the Holy Spirit that the mystery of God's Trinitarian essence attains its full profundity and clarity."[54] While generally speaking Barth is not known as a pneumatologist—rather as a Christologist—particularly toward the end of his life the Spirit gained more and more significance. It came to full fruition in his (unfinished) fourth volume of dogmatics focusing on reconciliation and ecclesiology. He sets forth a robust pneumatological foundation for the gathering, upbuilding, and sending of the church.[55]

A dramatically different "turn" to pneumatology is offered by the Lutheran liberal theologian Paul Tillich, to whom pneumatology was not, as in tradition, only part of the doctrine of grace or ecclesiology. Instead it occupied an important, separate place in dogmatics. In part 3 of the three-volume *Systematic Theology*, Tillich offers a profound and robust pneumatology under the rubric "Life and the Spirit."[56] His main goal is not only to connect theology and culture—the main motif of this theology—but also to attempt to transcend the dividing line between the Spirit and spirit. For Tillich the Spirit of God is the life-giving principle that makes human life and the life of the whole creation meaningful and specific. Thus, Tillich was

> concerned with binding together God and the world, or more precisely, God as Spirit and the human person as spirit. Ecstasy occurs when the human being as spirit is grasped by the divine Spirit. For Tillich 'human spirit' means more than human nature and embraces the whole human reality: morality, culture, and religion. The role of the Spirit in Tillich's theology is neither the churchy Spirit of ecclesiastical piety, nor the experiential Spirit of pietism, but the universalist Spirit who bridges all the gaps.[57]

Toward a Holistic and Comprehensive Account of the Spirit

Widely regarded as the most significant and undoubtedly most widely debated living constructive theologian, the German Reformed Jürgen Moltmann has produced one of the most significant pneumatological works of the twentieth century, the 1992 *The Spirit of Life*.[58] He had of course touched on many pneumatological themes earlier in his productive career. In his *The Church in the Power of the Spirit* in 1975, Moltmann constructed a pneumatological and charismatic ecclesiology in a Trinitarian framework. He explains that the focus on Pentecost in the doctrine of the church is a result of Christ's journey from Easter (*Theology of Hope*, 1964) to Good Friday (*The Crucified God*, 1972) to the outpouring of the Spirit.[59] The Trinitarian foundation of pneumatology comes to the fore as Moltmann looks at the emergence of the Spirit out of the dialectic of the cross and resurrection. In the utmost moment of separation and forsakenness between Father and Son, what "proceeds from this event between Father and Son is the Spirit which justified the godless, fills the forsaken with love and even brings the dead alive."[60] The Trinitarian approach to the doctrine of the Spirit is further clarified and deepened in *The Trinity and the Kingdom*. The Trinitarian God is relational and communion oriented: "The New Testament talks about God by proclaiming in narrative the relationships of the Father, the Son and the Spirit, which are relationships of fellowship and are open to the world."[61]

A strong advocate of egalitarian relationships, openness, and inclusion, Moltmann also vehemently attacks the subordinationist filioque clause.[62] An alternative to filioque is a robust Spirit-Christology—or as he also names it, a "*pneumatological Christology*"—in which Spirit and Christ presuppose and mutually condition each other:

> Jesus' history as the Christ does not begin with Jesus himself. It begins with the *ruach*/the Holy Spirit. It is the coming of the Spirit, the creative breath of God: in this Jesus comes forward as "the anointed one" (*masiah, christos*), proclaims the gospel of the kingdom with power, and convinces many with the signs of the new creation.[63]

If Jesus' ministry was the function of the Holy Spirit, then it means that "where the Spirit is not active, Jesus cannot do anything either."[64]

Indicative of a pneumatology much wider and more inclusive than a traditional church-based doctrine of the Spirit is the programmatic statement in Moltmann's ecclesiological work: "The Spirit fills the church with the power of the new creation, its liberty and its peace."[65] This holistic and cosmic orientation is further developed in his doctrine of creation, with a telling subtitle *A New Theology of Creation and the Spirit of God*. The panentheistic turn is also intensified as the purpose of the theology of creation is to "discover God *in* all the beings he has created and to find his life-giving Spirit *in* the community of creation that they share."[66] To accomplish this, the typical Protestant "Christological concentration" has to be matched by "an extension of theology's horizon to cosmic breath" of the Spirit and the acknowledgment of the "indwelling divine Spirit of creation."[67] In biblical traditions, the German theologian notes, "all divine activity is pneumatic in its efficacy."[68] There is also an eschatological turn. Unlike the Old Testament, Hebrew theology of creation, a *Christian* theology of creation is less interested in the "protological creation" and much more focused on the "eschatological creation," which on the basis of Christ's resurrection looks forward to the final redemption of not only spiritual but also bodily life. "The power of the Spirit is the creative power of God, which justifies sinners and gives life to the dead. The gift of the Holy Spirit is therefore eternal life."[69]

The (original German) subtitle "A Holistic Pneumatology"[70] communicates well the main thrust of *The Spirit of Life*, namely, to construct a doctrine of the Spirit in support of life, growth, and development. In other words, Moltmann sees the Spirit of God at work everywhere there is promotion of life, growth, inclusivity, and a reaching for one's potential; conversely, whatever destroys, eliminates, frustrates, and violates life is not from the Spirit of God. Moltmann laments the approach to the Spirit in mainline theology that, on the one hand, tends to regulate the Spirit's movements within the confines of the church structures and, on the other hand, tends to limit the Spirit's sphere of operation to the work of redemption alone. In this outlook, the Spirit is "cut off both from bodily life and from the life of nature."[71] According to Moltmann, behind this reductionistic pneumatology is the continuing "Platonization of Christianity," which defines spirituality merely in terms of church life and individual piety. The filioque clause has bearing on this issue because it has caused us to consider the Spirit of God merely the Spirit of Christ rather than also the Spirit of the Father, the Spirit of Yahweh, who is the life-giving principle in all of creation.[72] Moltmann reminds us that in biblical understanding the word *spirit* does not denote something antithetical to matter and body; rather "spirit" in the Bible refers to life-giving force and energy.[73]

In his search for a new paradigm in pneumatology, Moltmann also makes use of a number of resources from different Christian and ecclesiastical traditions, such as the patristic pneumatology of the Eastern Orthodox Church, the pentecostal experience of the young churches, feminist and other liberationist theologies, and cosmic and "green" pneumatologies. Radicalizing the panentheistic orientation, Moltmann argues that if "God's *ruach* is the life force immanent in all the living, in body, sexuality, ecology, and politics,"[74] then it means that the God-world relationship should be reconceived in a new way. The expression that Moltmann uses to describe his panentheistic orientation to pneumatology is "immanent transcendence."[75]

A significant contribution of *The Spirit of Life* is a radically revised discussion of the *ordo salutis*. Whereas traditionally the order of salvation has been understood as the "subjective" reception by men and women of the "objective" salvation wrought by Christ, Moltmann's thoroughgoing Spirit-Christology breaks this pattern and makes the work of Christ and the work of the Spirit complementary and mutually conditioning. Furthermore, he puts the order of salvation in the perspective of the panentheistic, immanent-transcendence-driven holistic framework at the personal, ecclesiastical, sociopolitical, and environmental matrix. Moltmann begins the soteriological discourse with the consideration of the liberation of life by harshly critiquing the gnostic juxtaposition of "spirit" to "body" so common in Christian theology. This kind of dualism is totally foreign to the biblical testimonies that speak of the "love for life": "Love for life says 'yes' to life in spite of its sicknesses, handicaps and infirmities and opens the door to a 'life against death.'"[76] In keeping with this inclusive and holistic orientation, the discussion of soteriological themes such as justification speaks not only of the individual's justification before God but also of a life of justice and equality. In the context of the doctrine of sanctification, the need for honoring the sanctity and value of life is highlighted at the communal and cosmic levels.

If the whole world and cosmos are the sphere of the operations of the Spirit, then consequently, there is a need to radically expand the traditional notion of the "communion of the Holy Spirit" to encompass the whole "community of creation" from the most elementary particles to atoms to molecules to cells to living organisms to animals to human beings to communities of humanity. In this "fellowship as process," all human communities are embedded in the ecosystems of the natural communities and live from the exchange of energy with them. In others words, any kind of community of creation is the fellowship of the Holy Spirit, be it an ecological community, a Christian community, a community of man and woman, or even a self-help group such as AA or the like.[77]

Incidentally, the same year that Moltmann's pneumatological magnum opus was released in English, the pneumatological work of another German Reformed theologian, Michael Welker, titled *God the Spirit,* was published in German. Welker focuses his study on a careful reading of the diversity of biblical testimonies for a postmodern and post-Enlightenment world. In what he calls a "realistic" theology of the Spirit, Welker wants to listen carefully to the diverse, multiform testimonies about the presence and absence of the Spirit in the contemporary church and society as well as in the biblical canon. What he resists is any "numinous," abstract, metaphysical notion of the Spirit, so prevalent in much of theology.[78] Welker's pneumatology seeks to locate itself and resolve the apparent tension between, on the one hand, the apparent feeling of the distance of God in the modern secular consciousness and, on the other hand, the enthusiastic embrace of the closeness of God in the rapidly growing charismatic churches.[79] Carefully reading the biblical, particularly the Old Testament, narratives of the Spirit, he is struck by the ministry of liberation and empowerment of the oppressed and weak. As a result, communities are being formed as

> the Spirit causes the people of Israel to *come out of a* situation of *insecurity, fear, paralysis, and mere complaint.* . . . In a situation of powerlessness, in a situation where it is to be expected that each individual person seek his or her welfare in flight, in a situation of perplexity and helplessness, the bearer of the Spirit—more precisely, God through the bearer of the Spirit—restores loyalty and a capacity for action among the people.[80]

Along with Moltmann, the Lutheran Wolfhart Pannenberg is the most noted living constructive theologian at the international and ecumenical level. With many contemporaries, Pannenberg issues a warning about limiting the sphere of the Spirit merely to the interiority of personal faith:

> The Spirit of which the New Testament speaks is no 'haven of ignorance' *(asylum ignorantiae)* for pious experience, which exempts one from all obligation to account for its contents. The Christian message will not regain its missionary power . . . unless this falsification of the Holy Spirit is set aside which has developed in the history of piety.[81]

Consequently, Pannenberg sees the Spirit at work not only in redemption but also in creation, as the divine breath of life.[82]

Differently from Moltmann, Pannenberg has not produced a separate pneumatology. Yet his three-volume *Systematic Theology* is based on and develops a comprehensive and robust pneumatology as part of an integral Trinitarian vision. Each and every main theological locus is connected with pneumatological considerations. Take, for example, revelation. The book that launched Pannenberg as a young theologian into world fame was the 1961 collection of essays titled *Revelation as History,* in which he produced a programmatic writing along

with being one of the many editors. Whereas then he was critiqued for not pro-
viding a role for the Spirit in revelation, the mature Pannenberg sets the record
straight as he speaks of "the word of the apostolic message . . . [as] Spirit-filled
in virtue of its content" and therefore capable of imparting the Spirit. The apostolic proclamation "imparts the life-giving Spirit of God."[83] A well-known and
widely debated insight of Pannenberg is the linking of the Spirit with the "force
field" concept borrowed from contemporary physics: "The presence of God's
Spirit in his creation can be described as a field of creative presence, a comprehensive field of force that releases event after event into finite existence."[84]
Pannenberg sees in this parallel great potential for faith-and-science dialogue.
While the biblical view of life as the function of the Spirit of life and the modern
scientific view of life as the function of the living cell as a self-sustaining and
reproducing system are not identical, the move in contemporary science toward
understanding explanations built on movement and energy has provided theology new prospects. From a theological perspective Pannenberg surmises that the
Spirit as life principle corresponds to the scientific idea of force field.[85]

Indeed, Pannenberg defines the essence of the Godhead as Spirit and puts it
in a Trinitarian perspective:

> The essence of the Godhead is indeed Spirit. It is Spirit as a dynamic field,
> and as its manifestation in the coming forth of the Son shows itself to be
> the work of the Father, the dynamic of the Spirit radiates from the Father,
> but in such a way that the Son receives it as gift, and it fills him and radiates
> back from him to the Father.[86]

Whereas Moltmann pushes pneumatology toward a panentheistic slant, Pannenberg is more traditional in negotiating this foundational theological question: "On the one side the Spirit is the principle of the creative presence of the
transcendent God with his creatures; on the other side he is the medium of the
participation of the creatures in the divine life, and therefore in life as such."[87]

While earlier in his career Pannenberg had been critical of certain types of
Spirit-Christologies—for fear of adoptionism—his *Systematic Theology* offers a
thoroughgoing, biblically based, Trinitarian Spirit-Christology based on key New
Testament passages, such as Romans 1:4; 8:11–14, and the Gospel traditions
linking Jesus Christ with the Spirit.[88] Naturally, then, he also rejects the filioque
clause.[89] This rejection is also related to his efforts to establish a Trinitarian doctrine that facilitates genuine mutuality among the Trinitarian members.

Unlike typical Lutheran soteriologies, Pannenberg constructs a thick pneumatological account of salvation in a highly communal context as he places the discussion of the *ordo salutis* in the context of ecclesiology. Here is a profound summary:

> 1. The Holy Spirit is the medium of the immediacy of individual Chris-
> tians to God as he lifts them up to participation in the sonship of Jesus
> Christ and grants them, as a permanent gift, the Christian freedom
> that enables them to call confidently on God as "our Father" (Rom. 8:15)
> because the Spirit gives them assurance that they are God's children (8:16).

2. The Holy Spirit binds believers together in the fellowship of the body of Christ and thus constitutes the church as he is present to it as a lasting gift (1 Cor. 12:13). He is present to the church, however, through the glorifying of Jesus Christ as him whom the Father sent (John 14:16), and therefore in the proclamation of the gospel and celebration of the sacraments by which the Spirit draws believers into the fellowship of the Son and confirms them in it (17:21–22).

3. The fellowship of believers in the church is a fellowship that by the Spirit they have beyond themselves in Christ, just as each of them by faith is lifted up to fellowship with Christ and therefore, filled and moved by the Spirit, is beyond the self in Christ. Conversely, by the Spirit the future of Jesus Christ is already present to believers as their personal and common future of salvation (Rom. 8:23 [cf. v. 11]; 2 Cor. 1:22; 5:5). Thus the fellowship of the church can be a significatory prefiguration of the eschatological fellowship of a humanity that is renewed in the kingdom of God.[90]

Behind the prominence of pneumatology in soteriology is Pannenberg's introduction of the Spirit as an integral partner in reconciliation; this means that unlike in tradition, the Spirit is not simply introduced as the subjective communicator of the objective salvation wrought about by Christ.[91] Pannenberg also provides us with a profound discussion of the Spirit in relation to the church, sacraments, and eschatology. As said above, each main theological locus is connected with pneumatological consideration in a robust Trinitarian framework.

"Evangelical" Pneumatologies

In recent decades the term *evangelical* in North American parlance (and by extension in the wider English-speaking world, including the British Isles) has become a technical term referring to a conservative segment of Christian churches who want to hold on to biblical authority and classical Christianity as explicated in the ancient creeds and Protestant Reformation. While critical of liberal theology, the evangelical movement, which is transdenominational and global, is also to be distinguished from reactionary fundamentalism.

The late Canadian Stanley J. Grenz, Baptist by denomination and student of W. Pannenberg, was a leading constructive, evangelical scholar who dialogued widely with mainstream Protestant and Roman Catholic theologies. His widely used textbook *Theology for the Community of God*[92] outlines an irenic, ecumenically open-minded evangelical theological program. It discusses the Spirit in a fairly traditional way in relation to the Trinity, revelation and inspiration, *ordo salutis*, and the church. Another leading evangelical, the late Donald Bloesch, a minister of the United Church of Christ and Reformed in his theology, devoted one whole volume to the Holy Spirit in the seven-volume Christian Foundations series. In that volume, he continues developing his overall theological approach, which he names "Spirit-Word theology." While Barthian in his orientation, Bloesch also qualifies the neoorthodox dualistic account of the divine-human relationship:

> There is a theology of Word and Spirit, which I also call a theology of
> divine-human encounter or a theology of crisis in that its focus is on the
> divine judgment over human history. It does not claim to set forth a
> revealed metaphysic, but at the same time it does not shrink from engaging
> in metaphysical speculation, for the revelation in Scripture has profound
> metaphysical implications.[93]

If Grenz represents a "mainstream" evangelical position, and Bloesch, the
"dialogical" one, then the other senior theological evangelical statesman, the late
Canadian Clark Pinnock, is to be regarded as both the "revisionist" and charis-
matically sympathetic theologian in the camp. Throughout his long career, this
Baptist theologian pushed the boundaries of evangelicalism with regard to issues
such as revelation, theology of religions, and the doctrine of God. His 1996
Flame of Love: A Theology of the Holy Spirit may be the most significant pneumatological work by a contemporary evangelical. Similarly to that of Moltmann,
Pinnock's approach is both experiential and suggestive; it is also doxological:
"The Spirit is elusive but profound and worthy of adoration. If Father points
to ultimate reality and Son supplies the clue to the divine mystery, Spirit epito-
mizes the nearness of the power and presence of God."[94] Echoing the latest turns
in contemporary theology, Pinnock's pneumatologically grounded Trinitarian
doctrine is both relational and life-affirming. He speaks of "a cosmic range to
the operations of the Spirit, the Lord and giver of life." This Spirit "is the ecstasy
that implements God's abundance and triggers the overflow of divine self-
giving." Pinnock's vision is world-embracing:

> The universe in its entirety is the field of its operations, which are so funda-
> mental for Christology, ecclesiology, salvation and more. This is the power
> that caused Christ's birth, empowered him for ministry and raised him
> from the dead. None of these things are possible for the flesh. And the
> Spirit is present everywhere, directing the universe toward its goal, bring-
> ing to completion first the creational and then the redemptive purposes of
> God. Spirit is involved in implementing both creation and new creation.[95]

Echoing Pannenberg and Moltmann, Pinnock's evangelical theology highlights
the principle of continuity: the same Spirit that was instrumental in creation is
also instrumental in new creation:

> Only the Spirit who brought life to the world in the first place can bring new
> life to it. Redemption does not leave the world behind but lifts creation to a
> higher level. The Spirit has been implementing God's purposes for creation
> from day one and is committed to seeing to it that they issue in restoration . . .
> Spirit challenges everyone to relate to God by means of his self-disclosure to
> every nation in the course of history. God is revealed in the beauty and order
> of the natural world and is the prevenient grace that benefits every person.[96]

While Pinnock is not recommending that theology should replace the Logos
(Word) Christology with Spirit-Christology, he is calling for a balance. One of

the main reasons for this call is the prevalence of the references to the Spirit in relation to Jesus Christ in the Gospels. While there were valid reasons for patristic theology to concentrate on the Logos theme—if not for other reasons, then for the apologetic one—Pinnock believes we are in a better place to seek for balance between Word and Spirit Christologies.[97] One of the biblical themes helpful in rediscovering the role of the Spirit in Christ's life is anointing; the title *Christ* (both in Hebrew and Greek) of course signifies anointing.[98] For this Canadian Baptist, the Spirit is also the key for understanding the *kenōsis*, self-emptying, of Jesus:

> It is important to recognize that Jesus was dependent on the Spirit. He had to rely on the Spirit's resources to overcome temptation. He was weak and human and did not know the life of undiminished deity. He suffered real attack in the temptations and was not play-acting. It was not through confidence in his own power that he put himself at risk. Victory over temptation was not achieved in his own strength. He overcame sin by the power of God and in so doing modeled the lifestyle of faith for us all. Jesus surrendered himself in trust and conquered the powers of evil by the Spirit, as we all must. . . . He conquered in the power of the Spirit. In becoming dependent, the Son surrendered the independent use of his divine attributes in incarnation.. . . . [The miracles] are not evidence of Christ's deity but evidence of the Spirit at work in him.[99]

Another distinctive feature of Pinnock's revisionist evangelical pneumatology is the way it views salvation not only—or even primarily—in terms of the Western concept of salvation but also in terms of the Eastern notion of *theosis*. That turn helps theology speak of salvation in "relational, affective" rather than forensic and juridical terms.[100] Differently from most evangelicals, Pinnock speaks boldly for the "wideness in God's mercy"—as the title of one of his well-known books puts it—in relation to other religions. He interprets this pneumatologically and argues that salvation through the Spirit's ministry may be available to many more than traditional Christians and contemporary conservatives have believed. It is also understandably one of the most hotly debated aspects of Pinnock's theology: "Access to grace is less of a problem for theology when we consider it from the standpoint of the Spirit, because whereas Jesus bespeaks particularity, Spirit bespeaks universality. The incarnation occurred in a thin slice of land in Palestine, but its implications touch the farthest star."[101]

THE SPIRIT IN THE ECUMENICAL MOVEMENT

Undoubtedly, the most significant ecclesiological development of the twentieth century is the rise and growth of the ecumenical movement. While of course much older than the last century of the second millennium—think of only such great patristic writings as *On the Unity of the Church* by Cyprian—never before has the ecumenical consciousness taken shape in and led to such visible and concrete manifestations. Behind the emergence of the ecumenical movement in the forms of the World Council of Churches (WCC), and numerous ecumenical dialogues and conversations among the churches, is not only the missionary desire but also a heightened awareness of the role of the Spirit as the Spirit of unity. In the words of the Roman Catholic Paul D. Lee, pneumatology "provides a fresh ecumenical meeting-ground, especially as regards a theologically more agreeable understanding of the Church. The Spirit continuously brings to the Church hope, vigor, and new insights." Thus, Lee is confident that a "growing convergence in the theology of the Holy Spirit promises new breakthroughs."[102] Another Catholic, Avery Dulles, rightly remarked that the rules of ecumenical theology must be "biblically rooted, ecclesially responsible, open to criticism, and sensitive to the present leading of the Holy Spirit."[103]

Significantly, the Seventh General Assembly of the WCC in Canberra in 1991 focused on the Holy Spirit under the comprehensive theme "Come Holy Spirit—Renew the Creation."[104] It was the natural culmination of the Trinitarian-pneumatological awareness that intensified in the ecumenical movement after the important drafting of the basis of the WCC at the Third Assembly in New Delhi in 1961, when a new orientation for the WCC became clearly visible. The basis of the WCC was enlarged to envision an explicitly Trinitarian, doxological formulation: ". . . to the glory of the one God, Father, Son and Holy Spirit."[105] The preamble to the statement places the understanding of unity in a Trinitarian, pneumatological setting:

> The love of the Father and the Son in the unity of the Holy Spirit is the source and goal of the unity which the triune God wills for all men and creation. We believe that we share in this unity in the Church of Jesus Christ. . . . The reality of this unity was made manifest at Pentecost in the gift of the Holy Spirit, through whom we know in this present age the first fruits of that perfect union of the Son with his Father, which will be known in its fullness only when all things are consummated by Christ in his glory.[106]

For decades ecumenical theology has worked to come to a more adequate and balanced understanding of the role of the Spirit in the Trinity. As a result, a study project on the filioque has been very useful.[107] The spiritual, ministerial, and social implications of pneumatology have also received much attention in the most recent work of the WCC and sister organizations such as Faith and Order. In 2005, the Commission of the World Mission and Evangelization (CWME) held its latest world conference in Athens, Greece, under the title "Come Holy Spirit, Heal and Reconcile—Called in Christ to Be Reconciling and Healing Communities." With a membership wider than that of the WCC, including for the first time the official participation of the Roman Catholic Church, a number of pentecostal/charismatic and other "nonecumenical" churches were presented. "The Healing Mission of the Church" is based on a Trinitarian-pneumatological foundation:

> 37 . . . Jesus Christ is the core and center of God's mission, the personalisation of God's kingdom. In the power of the Holy Spirit, Jesus of Nazareth

was a healer, exorcist, teacher, prophet, guide and inspirator. He brought and offered freedom from sin, evil, suffering, illness, sickness, brokenness, hatred and disunity (Luke 4:16ff, Matthew 11:2–6). Hallmarks of the healings of Jesus Christ were his sensitivity to needs of people, especially the vulnerable, the fact that he was 'touched' and responded by healing (Luke 8:42b–48), his willingness to listen and openness to change (Mark 7:24b–30), his unwillingness to accept delay in alleviation of suffering (Luke 13:10–13) and his authority over traditions and evil spirits. Jesus' healings always brought about a complete restoration of body and mind unlike what we normally experience in healings.[108]

The conference expressed its firm belief in the ongoing work of the Spirit in the world for healing, reconciliation, and restoration:

> In ecumenical missiology, the Holy Spirit, Lord and life-giver, is believed to be active in church and world. The ongoing work of the Holy Spirit in the whole of creation initiating signs and foretastes of the new creation (2 Cor. 5:17) affirms that the healing power of God transcends all limits of places and times and is at work inside as well as outside the Christian church transforming humanity and creation in the perspective of the world to come.[109]

One of the themes widely studied and debated in the WCC has to do with Christianity's relation to other religions. A continuing work in progress, the statement "Religious Plurality and Christian Self-Understanding" also speaks of the critical role of the Holy Spirit in Christian theology of religions. The following excerpt highlights the ministry and role of the Spirit in the theology of religions:

> 32. The Holy Spirit helps us to live out Christ's openness to others. The person of the Holy Spirit moved and still moves over the face of the earth to create, nurture and sustain, to challenge, renew and transform. We confess that the activity of the Spirit passes beyond our definitions, descriptions and limitations in the manner of the wind that "blows where it wills" (John 3:8). Our hope and expectancy are rooted in our belief that the "economy" of the Spirit relates to the whole creation. We discern the Spirit of God moving in ways that we cannot predict. We see the nurturing power of the Holy Spirit working within, inspiring human beings in their universal longing for, and seeking after, truth, peace and justice (Rom. 8:18–27). "Love, joy, peace, patience, kindness, goodness, faithfulness, gentleness, self-control", wherever they are found, are the fruit of the Spirit (Gal. 5:22–23, cf. Rom. 14:17).

> 33. We believe that this encompassing work of the Holy Spirit is also present in the life and traditions of peoples of living faith. People have at all times and in all places responded to the presence and activity of God among them, and have given their witness to their encounters with the living God. In this testimony they speak both of seeking and of having found wholeness, or enlightenment, or divine guidance, or rest, or libera-

tion. This is the context in which we as Christians testify to the salvation we have experienced through Christ. This ministry of witness among our neighbours of other faiths must presuppose an "affirmation of what God has done and is doing among them."[110]

EMERGING INTERPRETATIONS OF THE SPIRIT FROM THE MARGINS

While Christian theology up until the last decades of the second millennium has been predominantly the business of white male theologians from Europe and North America, that one-sidedness is undergoing energetic challenging, balancing, and enriching as female theologians of diverse backgrounds—feminists (white women), womanists (African American women), *mujeristas* (Hispanic/Latina women), and others—have joined forces with other liberationists, such as sociopolitically oriented black theologians, as well as theologians with agendas such as care for the environment, in producing a more inclusive account of the Spirit. Calling these theologies interpretations from the margins is only half-truth: women alone outnumber men in churches, and often are the main religious educators at home.

A form of liberation theology, feminist theology speaks of the role of the Spirit as liberator, which is in keeping with the biblical prophetic tradition in which "the Spirit's presence is consistently linked with the power to denounce social wrongdoing, announce comfort for those who are suffering, and bring about justice for the poor."[111] The day of Pentecost is rightly hailed as the day when the liberating work of the Holy Spirit was manifest and visible. Both men and women, the free and the slaves, were recipients of God's empowering spiritual power.[112] Along with the liberationist impulse, several female theologians' way of speaking of the Spirit includes the qualities of beauty, intimacy, and shared love, as in the Roman Catholic Ann Fatula's account:

> We ourselves know this Spirit, just as we intuitively know the air we breathe and without which we cannot live, for the Spirit lives with us and is deep within us (John 14:17). Though we may not always realize it, we experience the Holy Spirit's closeness when we are near our loved ones and our life feels good and sweet to us. We feel the Spirit's joy, too, as we savor the perfumes of springtime, when nature all around us bursts into bloom. Even hard times bring us the Holy Spirit's fragrance, for all that the Spirit touches is anointed with joy (1 Thess. 1:5–6). . . . Nothing created—not even the greatest ecstasy nor the most exquisite tenderness—can describe this happiness which the Holy Spirit is at the heart of the Trinity. . . . The Holy Spirit of love . . . dwells in us as our inseparable and intimate friend, our beloved "Paraclete" and counselor, our advocate and helper, our comfort and consoler. This Spirit at the depths of the Trinity (1 Cor. 2:10) comes to live in us not in a shallow or superficial way, but permanently and in our inmost depths: "I will put my spirit within you" (Ezek. 36:27, 37:14). Through thick and thin, the Spirit abides with us always (1 Cor. 3:16; 6:19; Rom. 8:9, 11; John 14:16–17; 1 John 4:13). Dwelling in us

more deeply than we ourselves do, the Holy Spirit draws us to our own heart, to find within us the contentment we seek outside ourselves. As we experience the Holy Spirit's closeness, we begin to take joy in our own company, for we know that we are not alone. Enveloped by the person who is the Father's and Son's own love, we discover that even our bodies are the temple of this sweet Spirit (1 Cor 6:19). . . . The Spirit unites us so intimately with Jesus that we now have a radically new power to pray (Rom 8:26), and to address the first divine person with the same intimate name which Jesus himself used when praying, "*Abba*" (Gal 4:6). No longer strangers and slaves filled with the spirit of fear, we are sons and daughters of the Father, filled with the Holy Spirit of God (Rom 8:15–16).[113]

The feminist theologians' focus on the feminine or maternal characteristics of the Holy Spirit helps counterbalance masculine pronouns for Father and Son. This is of course nothing foreign to Christian tradition. Applying feminine images to the Spirit is biblically legitimate, since in the Bible the role of the Spirit involves activities more usually associated with maternity and femininity in general: inspiring, helping, supporting, enveloping, bringing to birth. Of all the Trinitarian persons, the Holy Spirit is more often related to intimacy. Rosemary Radford Ruether reminds us that the "identification of the roles of Wisdom with a masculine Logos-Christ . . . largely repressed any development of a female personification of the divine, based on the figure of Wisdom, in the writings of church fathers."[114] Both biblical and early Christian tradition could also support the feminine understanding of Wisdom as seen in the book of Proverbs.

One of the complementary names for the Holy Spirit that Johnson takes from Christian tradition is Spirit-Sophia. It helps highlight many of the features of the Holy Spirit otherwise in danger of being neglected because the works of the Spirit-Sophia cover the whole of creation.[115] The comprehensive, universal role of the Spirit in the economy of salvation is also highlighted by another Catholic, the late Trinitarian theologian Catherine Mowry LaCugna:

The Spirit is involved in every operation of God in the economy. The Spirit hovered over the waters at creation; the Spirit spoke through the prophets. Jesus was conceived, anointed, led, accompanied, inspired by the Spirit. Only in the Spirit can we confess Jesus as Lord; the Spirit makes us holy and enables our praise of God. The Spirit gathers together what has been sundered—races, nations, persons. The Spirit is God's power active in creation, history, personality. The Spirit who animates the praise of God incorporates persons into the deepest regions of divine life. We must continually remind ourselves that this divine life is bestowed and active in history and human personality, not locked up in itself.[116]

An essential aspect of the world-embracing, holistic, and inclusive account of the Spirit's work in life is the Spirit's role in the environment and nature:

Of all the activities that theology attributes to the Spirit, the most significant is this: the Spirit is the creative origin of all life. In the words of the

Nicene Creed, the Spirit is *vivificantem*, vivifier or life-giver. This designation refers to creation not just at the beginning of time but continuously: the Spirit is the unceasing, dynamic flow of divine power that sustains the universe, bringing forth life.[117]

Elizabeth Johnson appeals to Christians to see the ministry of the Spirit—the same Spirit that raised Jesus Christ to new, incorruptible life—also in the natural sphere, particularly in the midst of the "damaged earth, violent and unjust social structures, the lonely and broken heart" all of whom "cry out for a fresh start." The Creator Spirit comes to this suffering, abyss, and devastation "to wash what is unclean; to pour water upon what is drought-stricken; to heal what is hurt; to loosen up what is rigid; to warm what is freezing; to straighten out what is crooked and bent."[118]

Other "green" pneumatologists have joined in the common reflection on the role of the Spirit in renewing and preserving nature. Mark I. Wallace's *Fragments of the Spirit: Nature, Violence, and the Renewal of Creation*[119] argues that there is a profound change in the spiritual sensibilities of our culture: many people sense that we live in the "age of the Spirit." Wallace works hard to rediscover in the theological tradition resources for a green pneumatology based on the idea of a biocentric role of the Spirit as the giver of life. The Spirit is best understood not as a metaphysical entity but as a healing life force. He argues that if the Spirit and the earth condition each other, then God as Spirit is vulnerable to the dramatic effects of ecocide. In his book *Finding God in the Singing River*, Wallace uses a striking metaphor when he wants to "retrieve a central but neglected Christian theme—the idea of God as carnal Spirit who imbues all things—as the linchpin for forging a green spirituality responsive to the environmental needs of our time." This is in keeping with the observation that the biblical texts do not "divorce the spiritual from the earthly, but, moreover, they figure the Spirit as a creaturely life-form interpenetrated by the material world."[120]

Other alternative and complementary approaches to pneumatology can be found in contemporary theology, such as the politically oriented *God's Spirit: Transforming a World in Crisis* by Geiko Mueller-Fahrenholz[121] and *Work in the Spirit* by Miroslav Volf,[122] which relate pneumatological discussion to political realities and to work. A distinctive feature of Volf's volume is that it also interacts with the Marxist understanding of work and society. Yet another example of emerging pneumatological paradigms is offered by John Polkinghorne, the Anglican clergyman and particle physicist from England who for years has reflected on the relationship between science and faith. He speaks of the hidden presence of the Spirit of God in the world created by God. In this understanding, "the sanctifying work of the Spirit is a continuing activity that awaits its final completion in the creation of the community of the redeemed, a consummation that will be manifested fully only at the eschaton." On this basis, Polkinghorne is convinced that some kind of congruence between the insights of science and theology are on the horizon.[123]

TESTIMONIES FROM THE GLOBAL SOUTH

Christian theology can no longer be done only from the perspective of Euro-American cultures. The majority of all Christians can be found in the Global South, in the continents of Asia, Africa, and Latin America. While academic theology is still dominated by views of (mostly) white (male) theologians with strong European flavor, a burgeoning theological creativity is happening all over the world as theologians from Asia, Africa, and Latin America join the conversation and help the global church to come to a more adequate and inclusive understanding of theology.

The Spirit of Liberation: Latin American Interpretations

The Latin American context is deeply shaped by not only folk religiosity but also the influence of Catholic piety and the rapidly growing pentecostal and charismatic movements, including those important to the Roman Catholic Church. Well known for feasts and parties, the Latin American continent has a number of ways of celebrating significant religious and cultural events. Not surprisingly, the Holy Spirit is the theme of one of the ancient feasts. The Feast of the Holy Spirit, or Espíritu Santo, is a communal celebration in which the whole population contributes and participates. The main ceremony includes the coronation of a child as "Emperor and/or Empress of the Holy Spirit" who then presides over a banquet of which all partake.[124]

While generalizations are just that—generalizations—there is much truth in the saying that whereas in Africa theology begins with a shout of joy, in Latin America theological reflection starts from a cry of despair. Another way of putting it is that while African theologians are drawn to issues of culture and identity, many Latin American theologians wrestle with social and political issues.[125] As the Roman Catholic José Comblin reminds us in his important work *The Holy Spirit and Liberation*, too often Western theology and liturgy have lost interest in the Holy Spirit, but "the new experience Christians are finding in those communities that aspire to the integral liberation of the peoples of the continent of Latin America is precisely an experience of the Holy Spirit."[126] While socially and politically oriented, liberation theology is essentially spiritual theology, as is illustrated in the book title of another Brazilian, Jon Sobrino, *Spirituality of Liberation: Toward Political Holiness*. "Spirituality is no less a prime dimension of the theology of liberation than is liberation itself," says Sobrino. "Spirituality and liberation call for one another."[127]

Several Latin American theologians have called the church to a renewed concern for the poor and underprivileged.

> Those who conform to the movement of the Spirit by forming communities made up of friends meeting in people's houses are the poor. Paul saw this happening in Corinth, and the same can be observed today. The ruling classes want a church organized from the top down; the poor want

a church built from the bottom up: they are the ones in conformity with the will of the Spirit. The Spirit works by founding new base communities, from which springs new life. . . . The clamour of the poor, the cry of the oppressed, rises up from them, and the Spirit is at the source of the cry of the poor (cf. Rom. 8:18–27). The church is the huge caravan of the rejected of the earth who call out, cry for justice, invoke a Liberator whose name is often unknown to them. . . . The Spirit is the one who gathers the poor together so as to make them a new people who will challenge all the powers of the earth. The Spirit is the strength of the people of the poor, the strength of those who are weak. Without the Spirit, the poor would not raise their voices and conflict would not raise its head. The antagonism between the people of the oppressed and the powers of this world (cf. Eph. 1:13–14; Rom. 8:18–27) exists because the poor exist as a people. The people of the poor cries out for its liberation.[128]

As is well documented nowadays, Pentecostalism and independent charismatic movements are the most rapidly growing Christian force in Latin America. At the same time, Pentecostalism is also influencing the Roman Catholic Church as well as most Protestant churches. An essential part of the pentecostal appeal in Latin America is the prominence of healing as a manifestation of the Spirit: "Experiences of healing are central in the Pentecostal understanding of the church and mission."[129]

The Spirit of Life: African Experiences of the Spirit

Differently from Europe and North America but similarly to the Asian and Latin American contexts, in African contexts religion permeates all of life. In the words of the premier Kenyan theologian John Mbiti, "There is no formal distinction between the sacred and the secular" or between "the spiritual and material areas of life."[130] For Africans, the world of the spirits is as real as the visible world, perhaps even more real. The visible world is "enveloped in the invisible spirit world."[131] Consequently—again, differently from the United States and Europe—life and world are believed to be governed by God, the ancestors, and (other) spirits. In many African cultures, living in a close relation to God are the spirits, including ancestors. Called by various names, these are real powers, created by God to mediate his power. Ancestor spirits, who are thought to live more closely to the living community than other types of spirits, are a central feature of all African religiosity. The implications for Christian theology and experience of the Spirit are obvious, as delineated aptly by the Nigerian theologian Osadolor Imasogie:

If the African finds his fulfillment only in relation to human and spiritual communities, then for him to feel at home in Christianity he must come to a vital appreciation of the role of the Holy Spirit as the unifying force in the Christian community. The solidarity of the Christian community inheres in the power of the Holy Spirit who unites all Christians with God and one another.[132]

In order for this to happen, the way of doing theology can no longer be decided by outsiders to African cultures. The modus operandi of doing pneumatology for the African context needs to be African.[133] Ironically, African theologians remark, much of theologizing in Africa, created and mentored by Christians from outside, lacks the vitality of pneumatology. A main reason is the secular and thus less spiritual mind-set of people, including many missionaries from the Global North.[134] It is also the reason for the "irresistible attraction of the modern pentecostal movement as represented in the Independent Churches in Africa." According to Imasogie, this attraction is connected with their emphasis on the place of the Holy Spirit in the life of the Christian. It also shows the failure of traditional churches to find a balanced, vibrant theology.[135]

Part of the African theologies' appeal to the Spirit is a kind of Spirit-Christology akin to that of the New Testament Gospels.[136] Donald Goergen believes that "an African christology ought to be a pneumatic or Spirit-Christology which shows Jesus' power over the world of spirits and his connectedness to the Holy Spirit."[137] Spirit-Christology and a pneumatological undergirding of the worldview, and thus theology, lead naturally to a holistic understanding of salvation. Salvation in the African context goes beyond a mere "spiritual" concept and includes physical and mental healing as well as deliverance from evil powers and spirits. As H. W. Turner remarks, it has been the role of the highly charismatic African independent churches to remind the rest of the churches of the importance of the holistic notion of salvation, which is different from the guilt-driven, individualistic, forensic notion of the West.[138]

In an important study titled *The Development of the Doctrine of the Holy Spirit in the Yoruba (African) Indigenous Christian Movement*, Caleb Oluremi Oladipo shows evidence of the vastly different notion of the role of the Holy Spirit among these West African people compared to Christians from the Global North, for whom the term "Holy Spirit" often denotes something remote and abstract. For the Yoruba, Spirit is "reality for everyone, as actual as the experience of being loved or the breathing of air." [139] Whereas in the West the Spirit's work is mainly conceived of in terms of individual salvation, for the Yoruba salvation, deliverance, healing, wholeness, including community wholeness and reconciliation, are also the work of the Spirit. Spirit is everywhere.[140]

A cherished metaphor in African theology has to do with ancestors. Not only have African Christologies and Trinitarian doctrines employed ancestral imagery; such images are also seen in pneumatology. For example, the Yoruba people conceive the Holy Spirit as the Grand Ancestor because of his role in sustaining as well as directing and giving spiritual guidance. In many African cultures ancestors exercise the mediatorial role and thus add to the feeling of solidarity and stability of communities. From a Christian perspective, the mediatorial role comes to the fore in the Spirit's ministry of intercession.[141]

The Spirit of Meaning: Asian Voices

In the words of the Sri Lankan Roman Catholic liberationist Aloysius Pieris, "The Asian context can be described as a blend of a profound religiosity (which is perhaps Asia's greatest wealth) and an overwhelming poverty."[142] Asian religiosity is rich and variegated and touches all aspects of life; in contrast to the Western modernist dualism between the sacred and secular, for most Asians not only is religion an irreducible part of all life, but it also undergirds beliefs, decisions, and behavior in everyday life. Even with rapid developments in technology and education, Hinduism, Buddhism, Confucianism, and a host of other religions, most of them manifested in forms that used to be called "animistic" (having to do with spirits), permeate all of life. Similarly to Africa, religion is a visible part of everyday life. Thus, talk about God/gods can be carried on everywhere, from the street markets to luxurious hotels to desperate slums to exotic restaurants. "The spirit-world is alive and is doing well in Asia," says Yeow Choo Lak.[143]

Similarly to their African counterparts, theologians from Asia have employed a number of pregnant metaphors and symbols drawn from their own soil to illustrate the nature and ministry of the Holy Spirit. Taoists characterize the Tao as "the receptiveness of change. Like the Holy Spirit, tao is patient and yielding. It changes, without intent, like buds opening. It accomplishes everything by inaction."[144] Another famous Asian set of concepts, yin and yang, has likewise been used in various ways. Yin, which usually denotes femininity in a mutually conditioning relation to yang masculinity—is an appropriate way of speaking of the Spirit as "she" in female and maternal images. Jung Young Lee writes that "the abstruseness of the Spirit in the Trinity has to do with her pervasiveness. She is present everywhere and at all times, and is known in both personal and impersonal categories."[145] The Confucian concept of chi aptly illustrates the cosmic dimension of the Spirit of God, animating and vitalizing all life, including the material body.[146] In several religious traditions, "bird" symbolizes divine presence and gentleness. The dove is of course also a favorite biblical symbol of the Holy Spirit. As Kirsteen Kim beautifully describes it,

> The descent of the dove on Jesus at his baptism is a reminder that, in Christ, God is reconciling the world (2 Cor. 5:19) and that, in the Spirit, heaven and earth are connected. Participating in God's mission is catching onto—and being caught up by—the wings of the Spirit as she moves in the world. . . . The mission of the Spirit encompasses the whole breadth and depth of God's purposes in the world.[147]

In the multireligious environment of Asian lands, the question of the relation of the Spirit of God to other spirits has become a burning issue. According to Stanley J. Samartha, Indian theologian and ecumenist and one-time director of the World Council of Churches' interfaith department, this question has "somewhat aggressively thrust itself on the theological consciousness of the church" in recent years.[148] Samartha notes that ironically, however, "in many theology textbooks, even those devoted particularly to the work of the Holy Spirit, one looks in vain for a careful, sympathetic, and extended treatment of the work of the Spirit in relation to the life and thought of people of other faiths, cultures, and ideologies."[149] It is to be expected that in the beginning of the third millennium Asian theologians will take leadership in helping the Christian church grasp in a more adequate way the complexities of "spiritual discernment."

Faced with the seemingly insurmountable challenges of this vast continent and hopeful of the unlimited power of the Holy Spirit, the Asian Bishops' Conference issued an urgent call for the coming of the Spirit:

> "Come, Oh Creator Spirit" (*Veni Creator Spiritus*) today is a hymn that swells up from the heart of Asia and finds expression on the lips of millions of its daughters and sons. As we Asians are facing the marvellous new things unfolding before our eyes today in every realm of life, we experience the irresistible power of that Spirit "blowing where it wills," crossing in one divine sweep, across all kinds of barriers and boundaries. The Spirit moves on, and in its movement it wants us to follow it, so that we may see, experience and savour the sublimity of the divine realities for which Asia has always been longing. It leads us, at the same time, to the arcane mysteries of all life in its every shade and form, filling our quest for the human and the cosmic with a new vigour and force.
>
> On the face of the Spirit, coming fresh upon us today, we recognise the power with which generations of our foremothers and fathers have been familiar during the millennial history of this continent. It is especially the life and experience of the poor and the marginalised peoples of Asia that has been much attuned to the world of the Spirit, as we find in their many religio-cultural beliefs, rites and expression. The Spirit binds us in a marvellous way with all those who have left the indelible imprint of their spirit, heart and mind in innumerable forms on our cultures and on our traditions. It is the same Spirit of God that Asia wants to rely on in shaping its future destiny. At the threshold of a new millennium, our Asian local Churches invoke the Spirit, knowing that its transformative and creative power is what we need most to be able to respond to the new and unprecedented challenges the continent is facing, and thus become truly Churches of the Spirit.[150]

Postscript

What Is New and Novel
in Contemporary Pneumatologies?

At every turn of the study of the history and contemporary state of pneumatology, one is reminded of diversity, plurality, and *creativity*. While an orderly account of the person and ministry of the Spirit is the stated goal of any introductory writing such as this, the theologian should resist all attempts to oversystematize a topic that by its very nature is dynamic, lively, and elusive. Rather, it would be useful at the end of this narrative to attempt to take a bird's-eye view of some of the defining movements, turns, and insights in Christian theology of the Holy Spirit. What are some of the ways the church and theology have come to a more inclusive, adequate, and comprehensive appreciation of the Holy Spirit?

In the past the doctrine of the Spirit was mainly—even though of course not exclusively—connected with topics such as the doctrines of salvation, the inspiration of Scripture, some issues of ecclesiology, and individual piety. With regard to the doctrine of salvation, the Spirit represented the "subjective" side of the reception of salvation whereas Christology formed the objective basis. In the doctrine of the Scripture, the Spirit played a crucial role in both inspiration and illumination of the Word of God. In various Christian traditions, from mysticism to Pietism to classical liberalism and beyond, the Spirit's work was seen mainly in relation to animating and refreshing one's inner spiritual life. While ecclesiology was usually founded on Christological foundations, the Spirit was invoked to animate and energize already existing structures. At times the Spirit was connected with various ministries in the church as well as with its prayer life and with sacraments—a connection made as a rule in the Christian East.

In other words, the role of the Spirit in traditional theology was quite reserved and limited. It is this reductionism that has been challenged in many ways by contemporary pneumatologies. While not leaving behind these emphases, today the Spirit is also connected with other theological topics, such as creation, God, Christology, and eschatology. There is an attempt to give the Spirit a more integral and central role. Political, social, environmental, liberationist, and other "public" issues are being invoked by the theologians of the Spirit in the beginning of the third millennium. The Old Testament idea of the Spirit of God as the Spirit of life has gained a new significance. Furthermore, contemporary theology includes a stress on spirituality. In contrast to traditional pneumatologies, often perceived as dry and abstract, there is a new appreciation of the experience and spirituality of the Spirit. Part of the desire to widen and make more inclusive the role of the Spirit is the attempt to find a balance between the principles of continuity and discontinuity. While, of course, there is no equating the Spirit of God with the human spirit or separating the work of the Spirit of God in the world from the special gift of salvation, contemporary theologians stress that neither should theology emphasize discontinuity in such a way that breaks the relationship between creation and new creation.

Finally, contemporary pneumatology also expresses a desire to connect the Spirit with ethics and life, an idea that is, after all, thoroughly biblical. Contemporary theology both acknowledges and desires to relate pneumatology to particular contexts, such as allowing women to express their experience of the Spirit in a unique way. Contemporary pneumatology gives voice to the poor and oppressed and to testimonies from Africa, Asia, and Latin America in a way never before done in the history of reflection on the Spirit. Last, but not least, contemporary theologies show an enthusiastic desire to connect the Spirit of God with the spirits of religions—in other words, to do theology of religions from a pneumatological perspective.

The recent rediscovery of the role of the Spirit has raised the question of the proper place of pneumatology in Christian theology. Traditionally, pneumatology has not received a separate locus in Christian systematic theologies. Pneumatological topics were usually incorporated into the doctrines of Trinity, revelation, and salvation (soteriology). Some aspects of the doctrine of the church also were usually connected with pneumatological themes—and that is more than understandable in light of the fact that in the ancient creeds, confession of faith in the Holy Spirit is part of the third article of the church, forgiveness of sins, and eschatological hope. A useful recent way to integrate pneumatology into the texture of the presentation of Christian doctrine is that adopted by the Lutheran Wolfhart Pannenberg, who in his monumental three-volume *Systematic Theology* connects the Spirit with each of the main loci of theology. In this approach, the Holy Spirit, far more than a "gap filler," is a necessary part of the theological structure.

The fascinating narrative of the various turns in the development and growth of pneumatological traditions throughout Christian history shows clear evidence of the continuing dynamic and energy behind this doctrine. How else could it be? The all-present, all-permeating, and everlasting Spirit of God cannot be contained or limited by failing human interpretations. Studying pneumatology reminds me of a favorite theological biography, that of the late British missionary bishop to India Lesslie Newbigin, titled *Unfinished Agenda*.[1] That title is as accurate a label for the study of pneumatology as any: while making every effort to describe the marvelous ministry of the Spirit of God during history and the present, the theologian—at the end of the task—can only bow down in humility, reverence, and intense expectation and look forward to the mysterious and ever-creative ways in which the Holy Spirit continues working in this world and in the lives of men and women.

Notes

Preface

1. Veli-Matti Kärkkäinen, ed., *Spirit and Salvation*, Sources of Christian Theology (Louisville, KY: Westminster John Knox Press, 2010).

Introduction

1. Elizabeth A. Dreyer, "An Advent of the Spirit: Medieval Mystics and Saints," in *Advents of the Spirit: An Introduction to the Current Study of Pneumatology,* ed. Bradford E. Hinze and D. Lyle Dabney (Milwaukee: Marquette University Press, 2001), 123.
2. Ibid., 123.

Chapter 1: Biblical Perspectives on the Spirit

1. The main source in this section is George T. Montague, *The Holy Spirit: Growth of a Biblical Tradition* (Peabody, MA: Hendrickson, 1994); for shorter, less technical discussions, see George Montague, "The Fire in the Word: The Holy Spirit in Scripture," in *Advents of the Spirit: An Introduction to the Current Study of Pneumatology*, ed. Bradford E. Hinze and D. Lyle Dabney (Milwaukee: Marquette University Press, 2001), 35–65.
2. A helpful outline of Old Testament perspectives is offered by E. Kamlah, "Spirit," in *New Dictionary of New Testament Theology*, ed. Colin Brown (Grand Rapids: Zondervan, 1978), 3:690–93.
3. A helpful guide to New Testament perspectives is offered by James D. G. Dunn, "Spirit," in *New Dictionary of New Testament Theology*, ed. Colin Brown (Grand Rapids: Zondervan, 1978), 3:693–709.
4. The term "Spirit-Christology" can be understood in two interrelated ways: (1) as a general nomenclature (as here) denoting the integral connection between Jesus and Spirit; and (2) as a technical term referring to those (systematic) theologies of Christ and the Spirit that make this mutual connection a theological theme. Understandably, this perspective leads to more than one type of Spirit-Christology; one should then speak of Spirit-Christologies in the plural.
5. A massive study on Pauline pneumatological traditions is Gordon Fee, *God's Empowering Presence: The Holy Spirit in the Letters of Paul* (Peabody, MA: Hendrickson, 1994).
6. See, e.g., James D. G. Dunn, *Unity and Diversity in the New Testament: An Inquiry into the Character of Earliest Christianity* (London: SCM Press/Philadelphia: Trinity Press International, 1991), chap. 9.

7. Yves Congar, *I Believe in the Holy Spirit*, trans. David Smith, 3 vols. in one (New York: Herder, 1997), 1:65.
8. Ibid., 1:65–68.

Chapter 2: Developing Pneumatological Doctrine in the Patristic Era

1. Eduard Schweizer, "pneuma," *TDNT* 6:396.
2. For the slow development of pneumatological doctrine, see Yves Congar, *I Believe in the Holy Spirit*, trans. David Smith, 3 vols. in one (New York: Herder, 1997), 3:19–216.
3. Gregory Nazianzen, *On the Holy Spirit* 26 (*NPNF*² 7:326).
4. I am reminded of the following remark by Wolfhart Pannenberg: "The NT statements do not clarify the interrelations of the three but they clearly emphasize the fact that they are interrelated" (*Systematic Theology*, trans. Geoffrey W. Bromiley, vol. 1 [Grand Rapids: Wm. B. Eerdmans Publishing Co., 1991], 269).
5. From the Greek *hypostasis*, which here basically means "personal" or "something with identity." This term has a checkered history in early Christian theology, as will be noted in what follows.
6. Gerald O'Collins, *The Tripersonal God: Understanding and Interpreting the Trinity* (New York: Paulist Press, 1999), 23–34, 91.
7. *2 Clement* 14 (*ANF* 7:521). For such examples in Justin Martyr, see J. N. D. Kelly, *Early Christian Creeds*, 3rd ed. (London: Longman, 1972), 148.
8. *The Shepherd of Hermas, Similitude* 9.1 (*ANF* 2:44).
9. Justin Martyr, *First Apology* 33 (*ANF* 1:174).
10. Athenagorus, *A Plea for the Christians* 10 (*ANF* 2:133).
11. Theophilus of Antioch, *Theophilus to Autolycus: Book 2*, 15 (*ANF* 2:101); Irenaeus, *Against Heresies* 4.20.3 (*ANF* 1:488).
12. For the early history of the doctrine of the Spirit, see further, Veli-Matti Kärkkäinen, *Pneumatology: The Holy Spirit in Ecumenical, International, and Contextual Perspectives* (Grand Rapids: Baker Academic, 2002), esp. 37–46.
13. Justin Martyr, *First Apology* 13 (*ANF* 1:166–67).
14. The so-called *1–2 Clement*, i.e., *First Epistle to the Corinthians* and *Second Epistle of Clement*, are not so named because of knowledge of authorship but because of an early association with Clement of Rome, the third bishop of Rome after the apostles.
15. *First Epistle to the Corinthians* 45 (*ANF* 1:17); see also, e.g., *First Epistle to the Corinthians* 8 (*ANF* 1:7).
16. Ibid., 42 (*ANF* 1:16).
17. Ignatius, *To the Philadelphians* 7 (*ANF* 1:83–84).
18. Tatian, *Address to the Greeks* 13, 15 (*ANF* 2:70–71).
19. Called also *The Pastor of Hermas*.
20. *The Teaching of the Twelve Apostles, Commonly Called the Didache,* 11.7–12, in *Early Christian Fathers*, ed. Cyril C. Richardson, 176–77. http://www.ccel.org.
21. *The Shepherd of Hermas* 2.11 (*ANF* 2:27).
22. Ibid., 2.10.1–2 (*ANF* 2:26–27).
23. For a brief, reliable source, see William Tabbernee, "'Will the Real Paraclete Please Speak Forth!': The Catholic-Montanist Conflict over Pneumatology," in *Advents of the Spirit: An Introduction to the Current Study of Pneumatology,* ed. Bradford E. Hinze and D. Lyle Dabney (Milwaukee: Marquette University Press, 2001), 97–118.
24. Hippolytus, *Refutation of All Heresies* 8.12 (*ANF* 5:123–24).
25. Ibid., 10.21–22 (*ANF* 5:147–48).

26. For Tertullian's relation to Montanism and its potential influence on his theology, see Kilian McDonnell, "Communion Ecclesiology and Baptism in the Spirit: Tertullian and the Early Church," *Theological Studies* 49 (1988): 671–93.
27. *The Passion of the Holy Martyrs Perpetua and Felicitas* (*ANF* 3:699).
28. Tertullian's *The Soul* (#45) mentions the names of Perpetua and Felicitas, who suffered martyrdom in the reign of Septimius Severus about the year 202 AD.
29. Origen, *Commentary on John* 2.6 (*ANF* 9:328).
30. See, e.g., *First Principles* 1.3.2 (*ANF* 4:252).
31. Ibid., 1.3.5 (*ANF* 4:253).
32. Irenaeus, *Against Heresies* 4.20.1, 3 (*ANF* 1:487–88).
33. Ibid., 4.20.5 (*ANF* 1:488).
34. Ibid., 5.1.1 (*ANF* 1:527).
35. Tertullian, *Against Praxeas* 31 (*ANF* 3:627).
36. Ibid., 9 (*ANF* 3:603–4), quoting John 14:28 and 14:16.
37. Origen, *Homilies on Numbers* 12.1, referenced in Pannenberg, *Systematic Theology*, 1:272, n. 48.
38. Tertullian, *Against Praxeas* 7 (*ANF* 3:602).
39. Ibid., 8 (*ANF* 3:603).
40. Ibid., 2 (*ANF* 3:598).
41. Ibid., 25 (*ANF* 3:621).
42. Ibid., 3 (*ANF* 3:598–99).
43. Ibid., 2 (*ANF* 3:598).
44. Origen, *On First Principles*, 1.3.7 (*ANF* 4:255). While this statement is in keeping with the later Eastern Orthodox tradition, ironically the background to this statement can be found in Origen's speculation about the different spheres of operation of the Trinitarian persons: the Father's in creation, the Son's in salvation, and the Spirit's in inanimate creation. This idea was supposed to guard the unity of the Trinity. Neither idea, namely, different spheres of operation and defense of unity on this basis, can hardly be sustained in light of creedal traditions.
45. Tertullian, *Against Praxeas* 8 (*ANF* 3:603).
46. Irenaeus, *Against Heresies* 3.24.1 (*ANF* 1:458).
47. Ibid.
48. Hippolytus, *Refutation of All Heresies* 1, preface (*ANF* 5:10).
49. Hippolytus, *The Apostolic Tradition* 2; 3.1–6, in *The Apostolic Tradition of Hippolytus*, ed. and trans. Burton Scott Easton (Cambridge: Cambridge University Press, 1934), 33–34.
50. Tertullian, *On Baptism* 4 (*ANF* 3:670).
51. Ibid., 8 (*ANF* 3:672).
52. Cyprian, *The Dress of Virgins* 22 (*ANF* 5:436).
53. Clement of Alexandria, *Christ the Educator* 1.6 (*ANF* 2:215). This work is also known by the title *Paedagogus*, a fitting name for a manual for Christian formation for those who have left behind paganism.
54. Ibid., 2.2 (*ANF* 2:242).
55. Irenaeus, *Against Heresies* 5.6.1 (*ANF* 1:531).
56. Hippolytus, *The Apostolic Tradition* 1.1, in Easton, *Apostolic Tradition of Hippolytus*, 33.
57. To talk about spiritual manifestations in Tertullian is a notorious task because of his association with Montanism (a topic to be discussed in what follows).
58. Tertullian, *The Soul* 9 (*ANF* 3:188); for Origen's listing and explanation of the gifts, see *On First Principles* 2.7.3 (*ANF* 4:284–85).
59. Tertullian, *Against Marcion* 5.8 (*ANF* 3:446–47).

60. Origen, *Against Celsus* 1.2 (*ANF* 4:397–98).

61. Cyprian, *The Unity of the Catholic Church* 6 (*ANF* 5:423): "He who breaks the peace and the concord of Christ, does so in opposition to Christ; he who gathereth elsewhere than in the Church, scatters the Church of Christ. The Lord says, 'I and the Father are one'; and again it is written of the Father, and of the Son, and of the Holy Spirit, 'And these three are one.'"

62. Ibid., 9 (*ANF* 5:424); In addition to the dove, a biblical symbol of the Spirit, Cyprian also refers in this passage to the gentleness and meekness of lambs and sheep.

63. Eastern Christian traditions of course include others than those mentioned above, such as the East Syrian (Assyrian) Church and several non-Chalcedonian churches (Armenian, Coptic, Ethiopian), and Jacobite (West Syrian) churches. This survey hardly includes them, except for the Egyptian Pseudo-Macarius and the Jacobite Ephrem the Syrian because of their profound influence in the Eastern Church and beyond.

64. *The Letters of St. Athanasius Concerning the Holy Spirit*, trans. with Introduction and Notes, C.R.B. Shapland (London: The Epworth Press, 1951).

65. Basil, *On the Holy Spirit* 11.27 (*NPNF*² 8:17–18).

66. Ibid., 19.49 (*NPNF*² 8:30–31).

67. Ibid., 6.13–7.17 (*NPNF*² 8:8–11).

68. Gregory of Nyssa, *On the Holy Spirit against the Followers of Macedonius* (*NPNF*² 5:323).

69. A telling example is this long listing of titles, descriptions, and nomenclatures for the Holy Spirit: "the Spirit of God, the Spirit of Christ, the Mind of Christ, the Spirit of The Lord, and Himself The Lord, the Spirit of Adoption, of Truth, of Liberty; the Spirit of Wisdom, of Understanding, of Counsel, of Might, of Knowledge." Gregory Nazianzen, *On the Holy Spirit* 29 (*NPNF*² 7:327). Other similar examples from Gregory include *Oration* 41: *On Pentecost* 11 (*NPNF*² 7:382) and *Oration* 41: *On Pentecost* 14 (*NPNF*² 7:384).

70. Gregory Nazianzen, *On the Holy Spirit*, 28 (*NPNF*² 7:327).

71. Basil, *On the Holy Spirit* 19.48 (*NPNF*² 8:30).

72. Ibid., 1.3 (*NPNF*² 8:3).

73. For a helpful discussion, see J. N. D. Kelly, *Early Christian Doctrines* (New York: Harper & Row 1978), 258–63, and Robert Letham, *The Holy Trinity: In Scripture, History, Theology, and Worship* (Phillipsburg, NJ: P&R Publishing, 2004), 149–51. Important contributions to emerging pneumatological doctrine came also from Gregory of Nazianzus, who in his *Orations* (esp. 29, 30, and 31) discusses widely the deity of the Spirit and the Spirit in relation to Father and Son. For a helpful discussion, see Letham, *The Holy Trinity*, 159–64.

74. Cyril, *Catechetical Lectures* 4.16 (*NPNF*² 7:23).

75. Athanasius, *Letters to Serapion on the Holy Spirit* 1.20, in *Athanasius*, trans. and ed. Khaled Anatolios (London: Routledge, 2004), 178. For the Spirit's role in the Trinity in Athanasian theology, see Letham, *The Holy Trinity*, 141–44.

76. Athanasius, *Letters to Serapion* 1.20, in Anatolios, ed., *Athanasius*, 219. A strong defense of the unity of the Trinity and the Spirit's role therein can also be found in Gregory of Nyssa, *On 'Not Three Gods'* (*NPNF*² 5:334).

77. Gregory of Nazianzus, *On the Holy Spirit* 4 (*NPNF*² 7:318–19).

78. Athanasius, *Letters to Serapion* 1.21, in *Anatolios*, ed., Athanasius, 220–21.

79. Kelly, *Early Christian Doctrines*, 257. The following references to Athanasius are provided by Kelly from Athanasius, *Letters to Serapion* 1.21; 1.22–27; 1.2; 1.20; 3.7; 1.25; 3.2, respectively.

80. Basil, *On the Holy Spirit*, 18.46 (*NPNF*[2] 8:28–29). For a strong defense of the full equality of the Spirit in the Trinity, see also Gregory of Nyssa, *On the Holy Spirit against the Followers of Macedonius* (*NPNF*[2] 5.315–28).
81. Basil, *On the Holy Spirit* 21.52 (*NPNF*[2] 8:33–34).
82. Cyril, *Catechetical Lectures* 4.17 (*NPNF*[2] 7:23).
83. Ibid., 16.11 (*NPNF*[2] 7:117); Basil lists a number of his predecessors whom he finds supporting his teaching, such as Irenaeus, Clement of Rome, Origen, and many more (*On the Holy Spirit* 29.71–74 [*NPNF*[2] 8:45–47]).
84. Ephrem the Syrian, *Eighty Rhythms upon the Faith, against the Disputers* 18.1; in *Selected Works of S. Ephrem the Syrian*, ed. J. B. Morris (Oxford: John Henry Parker/London: F. & J. Rivington, 1847), 165–66. Also known as Ephrem (or Ephraem or, named by Pope Benedict XV in 1920, the "Doctor of the Church"), Ephraim is the leading Syrian spiritual writer.
85. Ibid., 73.1, in Morris, ed., *Selected Works*, 339.
86. Athanasius, *Letters to Serapion* 1.19–20, in Anatolios, ed., *Athanasius*, 217–18.
87. Gregory of Nazianzus, *Oration 41: On Pentecost* 14 (*NPNF*[2] 7:384).
88. Gregory of Nyssa, *On the Holy Spirit* (*NPNF*[2] 5:321).
89. Basil, *On the Holy Spirit*, 18.47 (*NPNF*[2] 8:29).
90. Cyril, *Catechetical Lectures* 16.16 (*NPNF*[2] 7:119).
91. Athanasius, *Letters to Serapion* 1.24 in Anatolios, ed., *Athanasius*, 223. Biblical passages invoked in this paragraph are 1 Cor. 3:16, 17 and 1 John 4:13.
92. Basil, *Letter 105* (*NPNF*[2] 8:186).
93. Basil, *On the Holy Spirit* 15.36 (*NPNF*[2] 8:22).
94. Cyril, *Catechetical Lectures* 3.3 (*NPNF*[2] 7:14–15).
95. Ibid., 3.11–14 (*NPNF*[2] 7:16–17); Athanasius, *Four Discourses against the Arians* 1.12.46–47 (*NPNF*[2] 4:333); Gregory of Nyssa, *On the Baptism of Christ* (*NPNF*[2] 5:174–80).
96. Pseudo-Macarius, *The Fifty Spiritual Homilies* 9.7, 10; in Pseudo-Macarius, *The Fifty Spiritual Homilies and The Great Letter*, trans. and ed. George A. Maloney (New York: Paulist Press, 1992), 85–86.
97. Ibid., 19.1 (Maloney, 146).
98. Ibid., 23.2 (Maloney, 156).
99. Ibid.,18.5 (Maloney, 143).
100. The writing can be found in *NPNF*[2] 4. For an appeal not to undermine the role of the Spirit's gifts, see also Gregory of Nyssa, *On the Christian Mode of Life*, in *The Fathers of the Church*, trans. Virginia Woods Callahan (Washington, DC: Catholic University of America Press, 1947–), 58:141–42.
101. *Oration 18: On the Death of his Father* 28–31 (*NPNF*[2] 7:263–64).
102. Basil, *On the Holy Spirit*, 16.40 (*NPNF*[2] 8:25).
103. Ambrose, *On the Holy Spirit* 1.16.176–79 (*NPNF*[2] 10:113–14).
104. Ambrose, *On the Duties of the Clergy* 3.18.102–3 (*NPNF*[2] 10:84).
105. Ambrose, *On the Holy Spirit*, preface 1.2–3 (*NPNF*[2] 10:93).
106. Ibid., 1.8.99 (*NPNF*[2] 10:106).
107. Ibid., 1.9.100–107 (*NPNF*[2] 10:106–7). Behind this particular reasoning is an extensive allegorical explanation related to oil and anointment as types of the Spirit.
108. Hilary of Poitiers, *On the Trinity* 8.21–23 (*NPNF*[2] 9:143–44).
109. Ibid., 2.1 (*NPNF*[2] 9:52).
110. Ambrose, *On the Holy Spirit* 1.5.62–64 (*NPNF*[2] 10:101–2).
111. Ibid., 1.10 (*NPNF*[2] 10:108).
112. Hilary of Poitiers, *On the Trinity* 2.3 (*NPNF*[2] 9:52).

113. Augustine, *On the Trinity* 5.11.12 (*NPNF*[1] 3:93).
114. Augustine, *Tractates on John 105* (*NPNF*[1] 7:396).
115. Augustine, *On the Trinity* 15.17.31 (*NPNF*[1] 3:216–17). While Augustine's way of supporting the designation of the Spirit as love is somewhat complex here, the main point is clear: that as love the Spirit is what unites Father and Son. See also, e.g., *On the Trinity* 15.17.27 (*NPNF*[1] 3:217).
116. Ibid., 15.18.35 (*NPNF*[1] 3:219).
117. Ibid., 15.18.33 (*NPNF*[1] 3:217).
118. Ibid., 15.18.32 (*NPNF*[1] 3:217).
119. Hilary of Poitiers, *On the Trinity* 2.31–32 (*NPNF*[2] 9:60–61).
120. Augustine, *On the Trinity*, preamble 6.1. 22; see also, e.g., 1.2.4 (*NPNF*[1] 3:19).
121. Ibid., 1.4.7 (*NPNF*[1] 3:20).
122. Augustine, *Letter 169 to Bishop Evodius* (*NPNF*[1] 1:540).
123. Hilary of Poitiers, *On the Trinity* 2.26–27 (*NPNF*[2] 9:59).
124. Ambrose, *On the Holy Spirit* 3.1.1 (*NPNF*[2] 10:135).
125. Ibid., 3.7.44–47 (*NPNF*[2] 10:141).
126. Ibid., 1.3.40 (*NPNF*[2] 10:98).
127. Augustine, *On the Spirit and the Letter* 5 (*NPNF*[1] 5:84).
128. Ibid., 36 (*NPNF*[1] 5:98); see also 7–8; 5:85–86.
129. Ibid., 27–28 (*NPNF*[1] 5:95).
130. Hilary of Poitiers, *On the Trinity* 8.29 (*NPNF*[2] 9:145–46).
131. Augustine, *On Baptism, Against the Donatists* 3.16.21 (*NPNF*[1] 4:442–43).
132. Augustine, *The Enchiridion* (Faith, Hope and Love) 65 (*NPNF*[1] 3:258).
133. Augustine, *Sermon* 21.28 (*NPNF*[1] 6:328).
134. Augustine, *On Baptism, Against the Donatists* 5.23.33 (*NPNF*[1] 4:475).
135. *NPNF*[2] 14:3.
136. Known as Nicene-Constantinopolitan Creed, the basic outline of which was of course drafted at the Council of Nicea in 325.
137. *NPNF*[2] 14:163.
138. The Nicene-Constantinopolitan Creed as translated in R. P. C. Hanson, *The Search for the Christian Doctrine of God: The Arian Controversy 318–381* (Edinburgh: T. & T. Clark, 1988), 815–16.

Chapter 3: Experiences of the Spirit in Medieval Theologies and Spiritualities

1. For a helpful guide, see Stanley M. Burgess, *The Holy Spirit: Eastern Christian Traditions* (Peabody, MA: Hendrickson, 1989); idem, *The Holy Spirit: Medieval Roman Catholic and Reformation Traditions* (Peabody, MA: Hendrickson, 1997).
2. As indicated above, the nomenclature "Christian East" includes not only the "major" Eastern Orthodox churches such as the Greek Orthodox and Russian churches but also a number of other Eastern traditions such as the Assyrian Church, several non-Chalcedonian churches, including the Armenian, Coptic, Ethiopian, and Jacobite or West Syrian churches. In this survey, the smaller Eastern churches are only marginally represented.
3. The standard view is that this addition was first accepted by the Council of Toledo in 589 and ratified by the 809 Aachen Synod. It was incorporated in later creeds, such as that of the Fourth Lateran Council in 1215 and the Council of Lyons in 1274.
4. Against the standard view, Richard Haugh surmises that the addition happened just by way of transposition without any conscious theological reason. Richard

Haugh, *Photius and the Carolingians: The Trinitarian Controversy* (Belmont, MA: Norland, 1975), 160–61.

5. "Can a clause deriving from one theological tradition simply be inserted in a creed deriving from another theological tradition without council?" in *Spirit of Truth: Ecumenical Perspectives on the Holy Spirit*, ed. Theodore G. Stylianopoulos and S. Mark Heim (Brookline, MA: Holy Cross Orthodox Press, 1986), 32.

6. It is an established view in the East that the Father is the "source" (*arche*) of the divinity. In defense, see, e.g., Kallistos Ware, *The Orthodox Church* (New York: Penguin Books, 1993), 210–14.

7. Vladimir Lossky has most dramatically articulated the charge of "Christomonism" against Western theology. According to him, Christianity in the West is seen as unilaterally referring to Christ, the Spirit being an addition to the church and to its ministries and sacraments. Vladimir Lossky, "The Procession of the Holy Spirit in Orthodox Trinitarian Doctrine," in *In the Image and Likeness of God*, ed. John H. Erickson and Thomas E. Bird (Crestwood, NY: St. Vladimir's Seminary Press, 1985), chap. 4. See also Nikos A. Nissiotis, "The Main Ecclesiological Problem of the Second Vatican Council and Position of the Non-Roman Churches Facing It," *Journal of Ecumenical Studies* 2, no. 1 (1965): 31–62. All of these three objections—that it was a unilateral act, that it subordinates the Son to the Spirit, and that it compromises the Father's monarchy—were already presented by the most vocal critic in history, Photius, the ninth-century patriarch of Constantinople, in his *On the Mystagogy of the Holy Spirit* (Astoria, NY: Studien Publications, 1983), esp. 51–52, 71–72.

8. For an important Orthodox statement, see Nick Needham, "The Filioque Clause: East or West?" *Scottish Bulletin of Evangelical Theology* 15 (1997): 142–62.

9. So, e.g., Wolfhart Pannenberg, *Systematic Theology*, trans. Geoffrey Bromiley, vol. 1 (Grand Rapids: Wm. B. Eerdmans Publishing Co., 1991), 319. For a helpful discussion, see Lukas Vischer, ed., *Spirit of God, Spirit of Christ: Ecumenical Reflections on the Filioque Controversy* (London: SPCK/Geneva: WCC, 1981). Only a tiny majority of contemporary Western theologians support the addition. The best-known advocate of filioque was Karl Barth, who feared that dismissing it would mean ignoring the biblical insistence on the Spirit's being the Spirit of the Son. See Karl Barth, *Church Dogmatics*, ed. G. W. Bromiley and T. F. Torrance (Edinburgh: T. & T. Clark, 1956), I/1:480.

10. Boris Bobrinskoy, *The Mystery of the Trinity: Trinitarian Experience and Vision in the Biblical and Patristic Tradition*, trans. Anthony P. Gythiel (Crestwood, NY: St. Vladimir's Seminary Press, 1999), 302–3.

11. Symeon the New Theologian, *Symeon the New Theologian: The Discourses* 24.4, trans. C. J. deCatanzaro (New York: Paulist Press, 1980), 264.

12. Ibid., 33.1–6 (deCatanzaro, 340–44).

13. Maximus the Confessor, *Commentary on the Our Father* 1–2, in *Maximus Confessor: Selected Writings*, trans. and notes by George C. Berthold, Classics of Western Spirituality (New York: Paulist Press, 1985), 103.

14. Acts 17:34 mentions that Dionysius, a member of the Areopagus, was baptized by St. Paul in the aftermath of the apostle's famous speech at Mars Hills, the Areopagus, in Athens.

15. Pseudo-Dionysius the Areopagite, *The Divine Names* 1.1, in *Dionysius the Areopagite: On the Divine Names and the Mystical Theology*, ed. Edwin Clarence (London: SPCK, 1920), 51, http://www.ccel.org.

16. Also known as Maximus the Theologian and Maximus of Constantinople.

17. Maximus the Confessor, *Four Hundred Texts on Love* 87, 88, 90, in Berthold, *Maximus Confessor*, 45.
18. Maximus the Confessor, *The Church's Mystagogy* 23, 24, in Berthold, *Maximus Confessor*, 204, 207.
19. Maximus the Confessor, *Commentary on the Our Father* 4, in Berthold, *Maximus Confessor*, 106.
20. Maximus the Confessor, *First Century on Various Texts* 72–73, in *The Philokalia: The Complete Text*, vol. 2, comp. St. Nikodimos of the Holy Mountain and St. Makarios of Corinth, trans. and ed. G. E. H. Palmer, Philip Sherrard, Kallistos Ware, with the Holy Transfiguration Monastery et al. (London: Faber & Faber, 1979), 180–81.
21. See, e.g., *The Triads of Gregory Palamas*, ed. John Meyendorff, trans. Nicholas Gendle (New York: Paulist Press, 1983), 89–90.
22. Symeon the New Theologian, *The Discourses* 15.3, in deCatanzaro, ed. *Symeon the New Theologian*, 195–96.
23. Meyendorff, ed., *Triads of Gregory Palamas*, 33.
24. Callistus and Ignatius of Xanthopoulous, *Directions to Hesychasts* 5, in *Writings from the Philokalia on Prayer of the Heart*, trans. E. Kadlobovsky and G.E.H. Palmer (London: Faber & Faber, n.d.), 166–67; see also nos. 6, 7 (167–69) for a profound pneumatological sacramentology.
25. See, e.g., Meyendorff, ed., *Triads of Gregory Palamas*, 57–60.
26. Ibid., 66.
27. Symeon the New Theologian, *The Discourses* 6.6, in deCatanzaro, ed., *Symeon the New Theologian*, 124–25.
28. Ibid., 10.2 (deCatanzaro, 163).
29. Ibid., 1.5 (deCatanzaro, 45–46)
30. St. Gregory of Sinai, *Texts on Commandments and Dogmas* 41–44, 54, 56 (from *Dobrotolubiye*, vol. 5) in *Writings from the Philokalia on Prayer of the Heart*, trans. E. Kadlobovsky and G. E. H. Palmer (London: Faber & Faber, n.d.), 45–47.
31. Ibid., 128, 129 (Palmer, 69).
32. Maximus the Confessor, *First Century on Various Texts* 96–97, in Palmer, ed., *Philokalia* 2:186–87; Meyendorff, ed., *Triads of Gregory Palamas*, 52–53.
33. In Robert C. Broderick, ed., *The Catholic Encyclopedia* (Nashville: Thomas Nelson, 1975), 598–99.
34. Bernard of Clairvaux, *On the Song of Songs* 3.1, in *The Works of Bernard of Clairvaux*, vol. 2, trans. Kilian Walsh, OCSO, and Irene M. Edmonds (Spencer, MA: Cistercian Publications, 1989), 16.
35. Hildegard of Bingen, *Scivias*, trans. Columba Hart and Jane Bishop (New York: Paulist Press, 1990), bk. 2, vision 1, 150.
36. Ibid., 1.1 (Hart and Bishop, 67).
37. *The Life of Blessed Birgitta (by Prior Peter and Master Peter)* 22, in *Birgitta of Sweden: Life and Selected Writings*, ed. Marguerite Tjader Harris, trans. Albert Ryle Kezel (New York: Paulist Press, 1990), 175.
38. Ibid., 38, 40 (Harris, 82–83).
39. Julian of Norwich, *Revelations of Divine Love*, ed. Grace Warrack (London: Methuen, 1901), chap. 23, #49–50, http://www.ccel.org.
40. Joachim of Fiore, *Ten Stringed Psalter*, bk. 2, pt. 1, chap. 5, in *Apocalyptic Spirituality: Treatises and Letters of Lactantius, Adso of Montier-en-Der, Joachim of Fiore, the Spiritual Franciscans, Savonarola*, trans. Bernard McGinn (New York: Paulist Press, 1979), 125.
41. Ibid., 99.
42. Catherine of Siena, *The Dialogue*, trans. Suzanne Noffke (New York: Paulist Press, 1980), 141, 292.

43. Suzanne Noffke, OP, ed., *The Letters of St. Catherine of Siena*, vol. 1 (New York: Binghamton, 1988), 52, 161.

44. Catherine of Siena, *The Prayers of Catherine of Siena*, ed. Suzanne Noffke, OP (New York: Paulist Press, 1983), 158.

45. Noffke, *Letters*, 171.

46. Bernard of Clairvaux, *On the Song of Songs*, 8.2.2, in Walsh and Edmonds, eds., *The Works of Bernard* 1:46.

47. Meister Eckhart, "Grace" in *Light, Life, and Love: Selections from the German Mystics of the Middle Ages*, ed. W. R. Inge (London: Methuen, 1904), 4, http://www.ccel.org.

48. Meister Eckhart, *Sermon on Sanctification* in *Meister Eckhart's Sermons*, trans. Claud Field (London: H. R. Allenson, 1904), 41. http://www.ccel.org.

49. See, e.g., Bernard of Clairvaux, *The Steps of Humility and Pride*, 7.21, in *The Works of Bernard of Clairvaux*, vol. 5, *Treatises 2*, trans. Order of Cistercians (Washington, DC: Cistercian Publications Consortium Press, 1974), 49.

50. Stanley M. Burgess, *The Holy Spirit: Medieval Roman Catholic and Reformation Traditions* (Peabody, MA: Hendrickson, 1997), 70.

51. Aquinas, *ST* 1–2, q. 111, a. 2.

52. St. Bonaventure, *Breviloquium* 5.1.2, trans. Erwin Esser Nemmers (London: B. Herder, 1947), 141.

53. Ibid., 5.1.6 (Nemmers, 143).

54. Ibid., 5.2.2 (Nemmers, 144).

55. Anselm of Canterbury, *Monologion* 28, in *Anselm of Canterbury*, ed. and trans. Jasper Hopkins and Herbert Richardson, vol. 1 (Toronto: Edwin Mellen Press, 1974), 42–43.

56. Aquinas, *ST* 1, q.36, a.1.

57. Ibid., 1, q.37, a.1.

58. Ibid., 1, q.37, a.1; 1, q.27, a.4.

59. Ibid., 1, q.36, a.2.

60. Anselm of Canterbury, *Monologion* 50 (Hopkins and Richardson, 1:63).

61. Anselm of Canterbury, *The Procession of the Holy Spirit* 1, in *Anselm of Canterbury*, vol. 3, ed. and trans. Jasper Hopkins and Herbert Richardson (Toronto: Edwin Mellen Press 1974), 183, 191–92.

62. Bonaventure, *The Tree of Life* 3, in Bonaventure, *The Soul's Journey into God; The Tree of Life; The Life of St. Francis*, trans. and ed. Ewert Cousins (New York: Paulist Press, 1978), 127.

63. Bonaventure, *Tree of Life* 9 (Cousins, 133).

64. *The Venerable Bede: Commentary on the Acts of the Apostles*, trans. Lawrence T. Martin (Kalamazoo, MI: Cistercian Publications, 1989), 102–3.

65. Aquinas, *ST* 2–2, q.178, a.1.

66. Ibid., 2–2, q.171, introduction and a.1.

67. Ibid., 2–2, q. 176, a.1.

68. Venerable Bede, in Martin, *Venerable Bede*, 29.

69. The hymn can be found in Sister Jane Patricia, *The Hymns of Abelard in English Verse* (Lanham, MD: University Press of America, 1986), 84–85.

Chapter 4: The Holy Spirit in Reformation Theologies

1. The so-called Athanasian Creed is often known by the opening Latin word "whoever."

2. From German, the "Enthusiasts," Luther's term for the Radical Reformers, Anabaptists.

3. Yves Congar, *I Believe in the Holy Spirit*, trans. David Smith, 3 vols. in one (New York: Crossroad, 1997), 138. For a helpful guide, see Stanley M. Burgess, *Medieval Roman Catholic and Reformation Traditions* (Peabody, MA: Hendrickson, 1997).

4. For continuity with tradition with regard to the Trinity and the Spirit's role therein, see, e.g., Luther's statement in "Schmalcald Articles," no. 1, in *The Book of Concord: The Confessions of the Evangelical Lutheran Church*, trans. and ed. Theodore G. Tappert with Jaroslav Pelikan, Robert H. Fischer, and Arthur C. Peipkorn (Philadelphia: Fortress Press, 1959), 291.

5. Regin Prenter, *Spiritus Creator: Luther's Concept of the Holy Spirit*, trans. John M. Jensen (Philadelphia: Muhlenberg Press, 1953), ix.

6. John Calvin, *Institutes of the Christian Religion* 1.3.18, trans. Henry Beveridge (Peabody, MA: Hendrickson, 2008), http://www.ccel.org.

7. Luther, "Large Catechism," Creed, art. 3, #35–37, in Tappert et al., *Book of Concord*, 415.

8. Martin Luther, "The Sermons on Catechism," *LW* 51:166.

9. Luther, *Galatians Commentary* (1519) on 4:6, *LW* 27:290.

10. Luther, *Sermons on the Gospel of St. John* (1537), chaps. 14–16, *LW* 24:363.

11. Calvin, *Institutes* 3.1.3.

12. Luther, *Lectures on Genesis*, chaps. 1–5, on 1:2, *LW* 1:9.

13. Calvin, *Institutes* 1.13.14.

14. John Calvin, *Commentary on the Book of Psalms*, vol. 4, trans. James Anderson (Grand Rapids: CCEL, n.d.), Ps. 104:27–30, http://www.ccel.org.

15. Calvin, *Institutes* 1.13.14.

16. Ibid., 1.7.4.

17. *Huldrych Zwingli Writings: The Defense of the Reformed Faith*, vol. 1. trans. E. J. Furcha (Allison Park, PA: Pickwick Publications, 1984), 61.

18. Calvin, *Institutes* 1.8.13, 82–83.

19. Luther, *The Magnificat* (1521), *LW* 21:299.

20. Ibid.

21. Calvin, *Institutes* 1.9.3.

22. Luther, *Galatians Commentary* (1535), *LW* 26:375.

23. Calvin, *Institutes* 2.5.5.

24. Luther, "Schmalcald Articles," art. 8, #3–12 (10–11), in Tappert et al., *Book of Concord*, 312–13.

25. Luther, "Large Catechism," Creed, art. 3, #45, in Tappert et al., *Book of Concord*, 416.

26. Zwingli, *Defense of the Reformed Faith* 1:46.

27. Ibid., 1:57.

28. Luther, *Selected Psalms III*, *LW* 14:62.

29. For Calvin's teaching, see his commentary on Galatians 5:22, 25, in John Calvin, *Commentary on the Epistles of Paul to the Galatians and Ephesians*, trans. William Pringle (Grand Rapids: CCEL, n.d.), http://www.ccel.org.

30. For his commentary on Joel 2:28, see John Calvin, *Commentaries on the Twelve Minor Prophets*, vol. 2, trans. John Owen (Grand Rapids: CCEL, n.d.), http://www.ccel.org.

31. Martin Luther, "Small Catechism," Creed, art. 3, in Tappert et al., *Book of Concord*, 345; see also "Large Catechism," Creed, art. 3, #38–39, ibid, 415.

32. Zwingli, *Defense of the Reformed Faith* 1:61.

33. Calvin, *Institutes* 2.5.14–15.

34. E.g., Luther, *Two Kinds of Righteousness*, *LW* 31:298: "Through faith in Christ, therefore, Christ's righteousness becomes our righteousness and all that he has becomes ours; rather, he himself becomes ours."
35. Calvin, *Institutes* 3.1.1.
36. Zwingli, *Defense of the Reformed Faith* 1:57.
37. Luther, *Lectures on Romans*, *LW* 25:359.
38. Zwingli, *Defense of the Reformed Faith* 1:149.
39. For his lecture on Rom. 8:26, see Luther, *Lectures on Romans*, *LW* 25:365–66.
40. A clear statement of the Zwinglian position vis-à-vis the opposing view can be found, e.g., in Ulrich Zwingli, *On Providence and Other Essays*, ed. William John Hinke (Durham, NC: Labyrinth, 1983), 194–95 and 254–55 (in which he names the view of his opponents, i.e., advocates of classical sacramental theology, "sacramentarianism.").
41. Ibid., 114–15.
42. Ibid., 190; see also 109–10 and 254–55.
43. Calvin, *Institutes* 4.14.9; for a powerful statement on the Spirit's role in the Eucharist, see, e.g., Calvin, *Institutes* 4.17.10.
44. Ignatius of Loyola, *Spiritual Diary* 14 and 18 in Ignatius Loyola, *Spiritual Exercises and Selected Works*, ed. George E. Ganss, SJ, et al. (New York: Paulist Press, 1991), 241, 242.
45. Ibid., 109 (Ganss, 253).
46. Blessed John of Avila, *The Holy Ghost* (Chicago: Scepter, 1959), 9.
47. Ibid., 11, 12.
48. Ibid., 52.
49. Ibid., 46–47.
50. John of the Cross, *The Living Flame of Love*, trans. Jane Ackerman (Binghamton, NY: Medieval & Renaissance Texts & Studies, 1995), 70.
51. Ibid., 74.
52. Ibid., 82, 84.
53. St. John of the Cross, *The Spiritual Canticle* 25.7, in *The Collected Works of St. John of the Cross*, trans. Kieran Kavanaugh, OCD, and Otilio Rodriquez, OCD (Washington, DC: Institute of Carmelite Studies, 1973), 508.
54. Thomas Müntzer, *The Second Chapter of Daniel*, in *The Collected Works of Thomas Müntzer*, ed. and trans. Peter Matheson (Edinburgh: T. & T. Clark, 1988), 240.
55. See, e.g., Müntzer, *On Counterfeit Faith*, in Matheson, ed., *Collected Works*, 218–19.
56. See, e.g., Menno Simons, *The New Birth*, in *The Complete Writings of Menno Simons*, trans. Leonard Verduin (Scottdale, PA: Herald Press, 1956), 89–94.
57. For a standard orthodox formulation of the role of the Spirit in the Trinity, see Menno Simons, *A Solemn Confession of the Triune, Eternal, and True God, Father, Son, and Holy Ghost*, in *Complete Writings*, 491, 495–96.
58. See, e.g., Menno Simons, *Reply to Gellius Faber*, in *Complete Writings*, 760.

Chapter 5: Post-Reformation and Modern Pneumatologies

1. The standard—and most accessible—English source for Lutheran Scholastic theologies is the compendium by Heinrich Schmid, *The Doctrinal Theology of the Evangelical Lutheran Church*, 3rd ed., rev. and trans. C. A. Hay and H. E. Jacobs (Minneapolis: Augsburg, 1899).
2. The standard—and most accessible—English source for Reformed scholastic theologies is the compendium by Heinrich Heppe, *Reformed Dogmatics: Set Out*

and Illustrated from the Sources, rev. and ed. E. Bizer, trans. G. T. Thomson (London: Allen & Unwin, 1950).

3. Donald Bloesch, *The Holy Spirit: Works and Gifts* (Downers Grove, IL: Inter-Varsity Press, 2000), 113–14.

4. An example of ecclesiological topics can be seen in the discussion of the "perpetuity of the church" as the function of the continuing presence of the Spirit of Christ, in Francis Turretin, *Institutes of Elenctic Theology*, vol. 3: *Eighteenth through Twentieth Topics*, trans. George Musgrave Giger, ed. James T. Dennison Jr. (Phillipsburg, NJ: Presbyterian & Reformed, 1997), 44.

5. For Lutheran J. A. Quenstedt's formulations, see Schmid, *Doctrinal Theology*, 157–59; and for the Reformed ones, see Heppe, *Reformed Dogmatics*, 128–31.

6. For Reformed statements, see Heppe, *Reformed Dogmatics*, 131–32.

7. For statements by the Reformed J. Cocceius, see Heppe, *Reformed Dogmatics*, 17–18, and for Lutheran theologies, see Schmid, *Doctrinal Theology*, 45–50.

8. In Schmid, *Doctrinal Theology*, 45.

9. So Johann Gerhard in ibid., 55.

10. Heppe, *Reformed Dogmatics*, 23.

11. The main heading for pt. 3 of chap. 3, in Schmid, *Doctrinal Theology*.

12. Ibid., 409.

13. For representative views by J. A. Quenstedt, L. Hutter, Hollaz, and others, see ibid., 471–80.

14. Cocceius in Heppe, *Reformed Dogmatics*, 517; for other similar statements, see 518.

15. Schmid, *Doctrinal Theology*, 520; for the Reformed discussion along similar lines, see Turretin, *Institutes* 3:353–54.

16. Hollaz in Schmid, *Doctrinal Theology*, 540–41.

17. Richard Sibbes, *Treatises and Sermons from the Epistles to the Corinthians*, vol. 4, *The Complete Works of Richard Sibbes*, ed. Alexander B. Grosart (Edinburgh: James Nichol, 1862–1864), 205–6.

18. See, e.g., Richard Sibbes, "Description of Christ, Matt. XII, 18," in *Works of Richard Sibbes*, vol. 1, ed. Alexander B. Grosart (Edinburgh: Banner of Truth Trust, 1973), 17–19.

19. Ibid.,14.

20. See, e.g., Sibbes, "The Bruised Reed and Smoking Flax" in Grosart, ed., *Works*, 1:74–75.

21. Sibbes, "The Ungodly's Misery," in ibid., 1:392.

22. Sibbes, "The Difficulty of Salvation, 1 Pet IV.18," in ibid., 1:39.

23. John Owens, *Of Communion with God the Father, Son and Holy Ghost* (Edinburgh: Banner of Truth Trust, 1967), 17, http://www.ccel.org.

24. Ibid., 228.

25. John Owen, *A Discourse Concerning the Holy Spirit* (Edinburgh: Banner of Trust, 1965), 20–22, http://www.ccel.org; emphasis added.

26. Ibid., 94; see also 93–103.

27. Thomas Goodwin, *The Work of the Holy Ghost in Our Salvation*, vol. 6, *The Works of Thomas Goodwin*, ed. Thomas Smith (Edinburgh: James Nichol, 1863).

28. John Bunyan, *Grace Abounding to the Chief of Sinners* (Grand Rapids: Zondervan, 1948).

29. Charles Haddon Spurgeon, "The Holy Ghost—The Great Teacher," sermon 50, http://www.spurgeon.org/sermons/0050.htm.

30. Peter Erb, introduction to *Johann Arndt: True Christianity*, ed. Peter Erb (New York: Paulist Press, 1979), 1.

31. Johann Arndt, *True Christianity*, ed. Peter Erb (New York: Paulist Press, 1979), 37.
32. Ibid., 37–38.
33. Ibid., 252; see also 253–56.
34. Drawing from various influences, such as Neoplatonist and alchemical writers as well as, say, the Religious Society of Friends and Theosophy, Jacob's Mariology and theology of the incarnation clearly reflects his revisionist Christian cosmology and spirituality.
35. Jacob Böhme, *The Incarnation of Jesus Christ*, pt. 2, chap. 7, nos. 3, 7–8, trans. John Rolleston Earle, http://www.heiligeteksten.nl/THE%20INCARNATION%20OF%20CHRIST-%20BOHME.htm.
36. Philip Jacob Spener, *Pia Desideria*, ed. Theodore G. Tappert (Philadelphia: Fortress Press, 1964), 46.
37. Ibid., 116–17.
38. Nicholaus Ludwig Count von Zinzendorf, *Nine Public Lectures on Important Subjects in Religion*, trans. and ed. George W. Forell (Iowa City: University of Iowa Press, 1973), 4–5.
39. See Vernard Eller, ed., *Thy Kingdom Come: A Blumhardt Reader* (Grand Rapids: Wm. B. Eerdmans Publishing Co., 1980), esp. 18–19, 34–35.
40. John Wesley, *The Journal of John Wesley*, ed. Percy Livingstone Parker (Chicago: Moody Press, 1951), chap. 2, http://www.ccel.org.
41. Wesley also paid due attention to the importance and meaning of the doctrine of justification. See, e.g., John Wesley, "Justification by Faith," sermon 5 in *Sermons on Several Occasions* (London: Wesleyan Methodist Book-room, 1771), http://www.ccel.org. Similarly, he preached on topics such as the "witness of the Spirit." See Wesley, "The Witness of the Spirit," 1, sermon 10, in *Sermons*.
42. Wesley, "On the Holy Spirit," 3, sermon 141, in *Sermons*.
43. Wesley, *A Plain Account of Christian Perfection*, in *The Works of John Wesley* (1872, ed. by Thomas Jackson), vol. 11 (pp.366–446). http://www.ccel.org, 431.
44. Wesley, Sermon 13: "On Sin in Believers," III.1, in *Sermons*.
45. *Fletcher on Perfection*, by John Fletcher, ed. Michael R. Williams (Salem, OH: Schmul, 2000), 9.
46. George Whitefield, "Walking with God," sermon 1, in *Selected Sermons of George Whitefield*, http://www.ccel.org.
47. Whitefield, "The Indwelling of the Spirit, the Common Privilege of All Believers," sermon 38, in *Selected Sermons*.
48. It seems that Whitefield would basically consider the miraculous gifts reserved for the apostolic era alone.
49. Whitefield, "Marks of Having Received the Holy Spirit," sermon 41, in *Selected Sermons*.
50. *John and Charles Wesley: Selected Prayers, Hymns, Journal Notes, Sermons, Letters and Treatises*, ed. Frank Whaling, Classics of Western Spirituality (New York: Paulist Press, 1981), 187–88.
51. George Fox, *An Autobiography*, ed. Rufus M. Jones, chap. 1, http://www.ccel.org.
52. Ibid., chap. 2.
53. Ibid., chap. 7.
54. William Penn, *Primitive Christianity Revived* (Philadelphia: Miller & Burlock, 1857), chap. 1, #4, 12.
55. Ibid. chap. 5, #1, 2, 35–38.
56. Jonathan Edwards, "Work of Redemption," 1729, in *Works of Jonathan Edwards Online*, ed. Harry S. Stout, Kenneth P. Minkema, Caleb J. D. Maskell (2005–), 1, http://edwards.yale.edu/ref/10781/e/p/1.

57. Jonathan Edwards, "Spirit's Operation, Conviction, Conversion," 1730, in Stout et al., *Works*, 1, http://edwards.yale.edu/ref/11006/e/p/1.
58. Jonathan Edwards, "Holy Ghost," 1728, in Stout et al., *Works*, 1, http://edwards.yale.edu/ref/10562/e/p/1.
59. Jonathan Edwards, "Sin against the Holy Ghost," 1730, in Stout et al., *Works*, 1, http://edwards.yale.edu/ref/11018/e/p/1, 2, 3.
60. "Idealism" in the technical philosophical sense means the primacy of the spirit(ual) as the ultimately real in contrast to, say, materialism.
61. For a succinct statement, see the earlier work of Friedrich Schleiermacher, *On Religion: Speeches to Its Cultural Despisers*, trans. John Oman (London: K. Paul, Trench, Trubner & Co., 1893), 36, http://www.ccel.org.
62. F. D. E. Schleiermacher, *The Christian Faith*, ed., H. R. Mackintosh and J. S. Stewart (London/New York: T. & T. Clark, 1999), 569 (§ 123.1).
63. Ibid., 574.
64. Ibid., 570–71.
65. G. W. F. Hegel, "The Divine in a Particular Shape," in *Early Theological Writings (1793–1800)*, in *G. W. F. Hegel: Theologian of the Spirit*, ed. Peter C. Hodgson, *Making of Modern Theology: Nineteenth and Twentieth Century Texts* (Minneapolis: Fortress Press, 1997), 64–65.
66. See Peter C. Hodgson, *Hegel and Christian Theology: A Reading of the Lectures on the Philosophy of Religion* (Oxford: Oxford University Press, 2008), 127–40.
67. Hegel, *Lectures on the Philosophy of Religion* (1824), in Hodgson, ed. *G. W. F. Hegel*, 244.
68. Ibid., 248.
69. For an outline, see Abraham Kuyper, *The Work of the Holy Spirit*, trans. Henri De Vries (Grand Rapids: Wm. B. Eerdmans Publishing Co., 1946), 295–97, http://www.ccel.org.
70. Abraham Kuyper, "Common Grace," in *Abraham Kuyper: A Centennial Reader*, ed. James D. Bratt (Grand Rapids: Wm. B. Eerdmans Publishing Co., 1998), 181.
71. Ibid., 174.
72. Ibid., 184–85, 169.
73. Kuyper, *Work of the Holy Spirit*, 48–49.
74. Ibid., 39.
75. Ibid., 135; see also 33–34.
76. Herman Bavinck, *Reformed Dogmatics*, vol. 4: *Holy Spirit, Church, and New Creation*, ed. John Bolt, trans. John Vriend (Grand Rapids: Baker Academic, 2008).
77. Charles Hodge, *Systematic Theology*, 3 vols. (New York: Charles Scribner's Sons, 1917), 1:156–57, 163.
78. Benjamin B. Warfield, "The Authority & Inspiration of the Scriptures" (originally published in *Westminster Teacher*, Sept. 1889), http://lion.cso.niu.edu:4480/~ulrick/christian/pdf/warfield/authority.pdf.
79. Hodge, *Systematic Theology*, 2:660; see also 2:654–61.
80. Charles Hodge, *The Way of Life* (London: Banner of Truth Trust, 1959).
81. A. A. Hodge, *Outlines of Theology*, rewritten and enlarged (Grand Rapids: Wm. B. Eerdmans Publishing Co., 1949), 174–76.
82. Benjamin B. Warfield, "The Cessation of the Charismata," http://www.the-highway.com/cessation1_Warfield.html.
83. Benjamin B. Warfield, *The Power of God unto Salvation* (Grand Rapids: Wm. B. Eerdmans Publishing Co., 1930), 134.

Chapter 6: The Spirit in Twentieth-Century Interpretations

1. Stanley M. Burgess and Eduard M. van der Maas, eds., *The New International Dictionary of Pentecostal and Charismatic Movements*, rev. and exp. ed. (Grand Rapids: Zondervan, 2002).
2. See Cecil M. Robeck, "Pentecostal Origins from a Global Perspective," *All Together in One Place: Theological Papers from the Brighton Conference on World Evangelization*, ed. H. D. Hunter and P. D. Hocken (Sheffield: Sheffield Academic Press, 1993), 166–80. For a helpful discussion of the pentecostal identity and specific features, see also Allan Anderson, *An Introduction to Pentecostalism: Global Charismatic Christianity* (Cambridge: Cambridge University Press, 2004), 13–14, 187, 196.
3. A definitive study of the main motifs of "full gospel" is Donald W. Dayton, *Theological Roots of Pentecostalism* (Grand Rapids: Zondervan, 1987). For a fine account of key themes and orientations in pentecostal spirituality, see Russell P. Spittler, "Spirituality, Pentecostal and Charismatic," in Burgess and van der Maas, eds., *New International Dictionary*, 1096–1102. See also W. J. Hollenweger, "From Azusa Street to Toronto Phenomenon: Historical Roots of Pentecostalism," *Concilium* 3 (1996): 3–14.
4. Harvey Cox, *Fire from Heaven: The Rise of Pentecostal Spirituality and the Reshaping of Religion in the Twenty-first Century* (Reading, MA: Addison Wesley, 1995), 81–82.
5. See further, ibid., 299–301.
6. See Frank Macchia, "Baptized in the Spirit: Towards a Global Theology of Spirit Baptism," in *The Spirit in the World: Emerging Pentecostal Theologies in Global Context*, ed. Veli-Matti Kärkkäinen (Grand Rapids: Wm. B. Eerdmans Publishing Co., 2009), 3–20.
7. For the term "Spirit baptism" and its various understandings in Pentecostalism and among charismatic movements, such as Roman Catholic charismatics, see Koo D. Yun, *Baptism in the Holy Spirit: An Ecumenical Theology of Spirit Baptism* (Lanham, MD: University Press of America, 2003).
8. Pentecostal biblical scholarship has devoted much effort in studying Lukan pneumatology. Some of the first studies were Roger Stronstat, *The Charismatic Theology of St. Luke* (Peabody, MA: Hendrickson, 1984), and Robert Menzies, *The Development of Early Christian Pneumatology with Special Reference to Luke–Acts* (Sheffield: Sheffield Academic Press, 1991).
9. See further, Amos Yong, "The Demonic in Pentecostal-Charismatic Christianity and in the Religious Consciousness of Asia," in *Asian and Pentecostal: The Charismatic Face of Christianity in Asia*, ed. Allan Anderson and Edmond Tang (London: Regnum International; Baguio City, Philippines: Asia Pacific Theological Seminary Press, 2005), 93–127.
10. Amos Yong, *The Spirit Poured Out on All Flesh: Pentecostalism and the Possibility of Global Theology* (Grand Rapids: Baker Academic, 2005), 82.
11. Yong, *The Spirit*, 38–39.
12. See the important study of the significance of eschatology to the formation of Pentecostal theology by D. William Faupel: *The Everlasting Gospel: The Significance of Eschatology in the Development of Pentecostal Thought* (Sheffield: Sheffield Academic Press, 1996). A definitive study with regard to pentecostal spirituality in light of eschatological expectation is Steven J. Land, *Pentecostal Spirituality: A Passion for the Kingdom*, Journal of Pentecostal Theology Supplement Series 1 (Sheffield: Sheffield Academic Press, 1993).

13. Amos Yong, "'The Spirit Hovers over the World': Toward a Typology of 'Spirit' in the Religion and Science Dialogue," *The Digest: Transdisciplinary Approaches to Foundational Questions* 4, no. 12 (2004), http://www.metanexus.net/magazine/ArticleDetail/tabid/68/id/9140/Default.aspx.

14. Anne K. Turley, "Articles on Aspects of Eastern Orthodox Christian Doctrine and Practices, Ecumenism, Contemporary Events, etc.," originally published with the blessing of the Most Reverend Anthony Archbishop of Western American San Francisco, http://www.orthodox.net/articles/heavenonearth.html.

15. Sergius Bulgakov, *The Comforter*, trans. Boris Jakim (Grand Rapids: Wm. B. Eerdmans Publishing Co., 2004).

16. Excerpt from funeral homily by Metropolitan Evloghios, http://www.byzantineimages.com/bulgakov.htm.

17. Vladimir Lossky, *The Mystical Theology of the Eastern Church* (New York: St. Vladimir Seminary Press, 1976), 158–59; John Zizioulas, *Being as Communion: Studies in Personhood and Church* (Crestwood, NY: St. Vladimir's Seminary Press, 1985), 126–36.

18. Georgios I. Mantzarides, *The Deification of Man* (Crestwood, NY: St Vladimir's Seminary Press, 1984).

19. Lossky, *Mystical Theology*, 168; for the "shyness" of the Spirit, see also Kallistos Ware, *The Orthodox Way* (Crestwood, NY: St. Vladimir's Seminary Press, 1979), 119.

20. Ibid., 179, 181.

21. See ibid., 156–57.

22. Zizioulas, *Being as Communion*, 131–32.

23. Dumitru Staniloae, *The Experience of God: Orthodox Dogmatic Theology*, vol. 2 (Brookline, MA: Holy Cross Orthodox Press, 2000), 60.

24. Ibid., 2:67–68.

25. All these encyclicals are available at http://www.vatican.va/holy_father/john_paul_ii/encyclicals/. References are to paragraphs rather than to page numbers.

26. An excellent discussion can be found in Thomas Hughson, SJ, "Interpreting Vatican II: 'A New Pentecost'," *Theological Studies* 69 (2008): 3–37.

27. Germain Marc'hadour, "The Holy Spirit over the New World: II," *Clergy Review* 59, no. 4 (1974): 247–48.

28. All Vatican II documents are available at http://www.vatican.va/archive/hist_councils/ii_vatican_council/. References are to paragraphs rather than to page numbers.

29. For a helpful discussion, see Elizabeth Theresa Groppe, "The Contribution of Yves Congar's Theology of the Holy Spirit," *Theological Studies* 62 (2001): 451–78.

30. For a discussion and assessment, see John R. Sachs, "'Do Not Stifle the Spirit': Karl Rahner, The Legacy of Vatican II, and Its Urgency for Theology Today," in *Toward a Spirited Theology: The Holy Spirit's Challenge to the Theological Disciplines*, ed. Judith A. Dwyer (Washington, DC: Catholic Theological Society of America, 1996), 15–38.

31. Hans Urs von Balthasar, *Theo-Logic*, vol. 3: *The Spirit of Truth*, trans. Graham Harrison (San Francisco: Ignatius Press, 2005), 223–34.

32. Ibid., http://catholiceducation.org/articles/religion/re0765.html.

33. Yves Congar, *I Believe in the Holy Spirit*, trans. David Smith, 3 vols. in one (New York: Crossroad, 2000), 1:65.

34. Ibid., 2:151–52.

35. Ibid., 2:67–68.

36. Karl Rahner, *Foundations of Christian Faith: An Introduction to the Idea of Christianity*, trans. William V. Dych (New York: Crossroad, 2004), 139.
37. Ibid., 120.
38. Ibid., 139.
39. Karl Rahner, "Do Not Stifle the Spirit," in *Theological Investigations*, vol. 7, trans. Cornelius Ernst (New York: Herder, 1971), 76.
40. Karl Rahner, *The Dynamic Element in the Church* (New York: Herder & Herder, 1964), 82–83.
41. Kilian McDonnell, OSB, "The Determinative Doctrine of the Holy Spirit," *Theology Today* 39, no. 2 (1982): 142.
42. Ibid., 142.
43. Kilian McDonnell, OSB, *The Other Hand of God: The Holy Spirit as the Universal Touch and Goal* (Collegeville, MN: Liturgical Press, 2003), 30–31.
44. Ibid., 34–37.
45. Hendrikus Berkhof, *The Doctrine of the Holy Spirit* (Atlanta: John Knox Press, 1964), 14.
46. Ibid., 69–70.
47. Ibid., 95–96.
48. Ibid., 104.
49. Geoffrey Lampe, *God as Spirit* (Oxford: Clarendon Press, 1977), 11.
50. Barth, *CD* I/1, 453.
51. Karl Barth, *Evangelical Theology: An Introduction*, trans. Foley Grover (Grand Rapids: Wm. B. Eerdmans Publishing Co., 1963), 53–54.
52. Barth, *CD* I/1:296.
53. Ibid., 299.
54. Barth, *CD* III/1:56–57.
55. Barth, *CD* IV/1–3 and 4 (which was not finished).
56. Paul Tillich, *Systematic Theology*. 3 vols. in one (Chicago, University of Chicago Press, 1961–1963), 3:11–294.
57. As explained by the Catholic commentator McDonnell in "Determinative Doctrine," 155.
58. Jürgen Moltmann, *The Spirit of Life: A Universal Affirmation*, trans. Margaret Kohl (Minneapolis: Fortress Press, 1992).
59. Jürgen Moltmann, *The Church in the Power of the Spirit: A Contribution to Messianic Ecclesiology*, trans. Margaret Kohl (Minneapolis: Fortress Press, 1993), xx.
60. Jürgen Moltmann, *The Crucified God: The Cross of Christ as the Foundation and Criticism of Christian Theology* (London: SCM Press, 1974), 244.
61. Moltmann, *Trinity and the Kingdom: The Doctrine of God*, trans. Margaret Kohl (San Francisco: Harper & Row, 1981), 64.
62. For details, see Moltmann, *Trinity and the Kingdom*, 178–87.
63. Jürgen Moltmann, *The Way of Jesus Christ: Christology in Messianic Dimensions* (Minneapolis: Fortress Press, 1993), 73.
64. Ibid., 91. "We have . . . to talk about a *kenosis of the Holy Spirit*, which emptied itself and descended from the eternity of God, taking up its dwelling in this vulnerable and moral human being Jesus" (ibid., 93).
65. Moltmann, *Church in the Power*, xviii.
66. Jürgen Moltmann, *God in Creation: A New Theology of Creation and the Spirit of God*, trans. Margaret Kohl (London: SCM Press, 1985), xi.
67. Ibid., xiv.
68. Ibid., 9.

69. Ibid., 96.
70. ET: *A Universal Affirmation.*
71. Moltmann, *Spirit of Life*, 8; also 2.
72. Ibid., 8–9.
73. Ibid., 40.
74. Ibid., 225–26.
75. Ibid., 35.
76. Ibid. 84–86.
77. Moltmann, *Spirit of Life*, 225–26, and chap. 11.
78. Michael Welker, *God the Spirit*, trans. John F. Hoffmeyer (Minneapolis: Fortress Press, 1994), ix.
79. Ibid., 1–2, 6–7.
80. Ibid., 56.
81. Wolfhart Pannenberg, "Insight and Faith," in *Basic Questions in Theology*, trans. George H. Kehm, vol. 2 (Philadelphia: Fortress Press, 1971), 43.
82. Wolfhart Pannenberg, *Systematic Theology*, trans. Geoffrey W. Bromiley, 3 vols. (Grand Rapids: Wm. B. Eerdmans Publishing Co., 1991, 1994, 1998), 3:1.
83. Pannenberg, *Systematic Theology*, 1:249.
84. Wolfhart Pannenberg, *Introduction to Systematic Theology* (Grand Rapids: Wm. B. Eerdmans Publishing Co., 1991), 194; see also, e.g., Pannenberg, *Systematic Theology*, 1:383–84.
85. Pannenberg, *Systematic Theology*, 2:76–84.
86. Ibid., 1:429.
87. Ibid., 2:32.
88. Ibid., 1:266–67.
89. Ibid., 1:318–19.
90. Ibid., 3:134–35.
91. Ibid., 2:450–53.
92. Stanley J. Grenz, *Theology for the Community of God* (Grand Rapids: Wm. B. Eerdmans Publishing Co., 2000).
93. Donald G. Bloesch, *The Holy Spirit: Works and Gifts*, Christian Foundations Series (Downers Grove, IL: InterVarsity Press, 2000), 45.
94. Clark H. Pinnock, *Flame of Love: A Theology of the Holy Spirit* (Downers Grove, IL: InterVarsity Press, 1996), 9.
95. Ibid., 50.
96. Ibid., 54, 61.
97. Ibid., 91.
98. Ibid., 79.
99. Ibid., 88–90.
100. Ibid., 149.
101. Ibid., 188.
102. Paul D. Lee, *Pneumatological Ecclesiology in Roman Catholic-Pentecostal Dialogue: A Catholic Reading of the Third Quinquennium (1985–1989)* (unpublished dissertation, Pontifical University of Saint Thomas Aquinas, Rome, 1994), 2.
103. Avery Dulles, "Method in Ecumenical Theology," in *The Craft of Theology: From Symbol to System*, Avery Dulles (New York: Crossroad, 1992), 195. In this sense we could criticize the model of ecumenical theology posed by Hans Küng for its total lack of pneumatological reference, as is clearly seen in his definition of ecumenism (found in Hans Küng, *Theology for the Third Millennium: An Ecumenical View* [New York: Doubleday, 1988], 169, 206).
104. For proceedings, see *Signs of the Spirit: Official Report, Seventh Assembly*, ed. Michael Kinnamon (Geneva: WCC, 1991).

105. W. A. Visser't Hooft, "The Basis: Its History and Significance," *Ecumenical Review* 2 (1985): 170ff.

106. "New Delhi Section on Unity," in *A Documentary History of the Faith and Order Movement 1927–1963*, ed. L. Vischer (St. Louis: Bethany, 1963), 144, # 1. Konrad Raiser ("The Holy Spirit in Modern Ecumenical Thought," *Ecumenical Review* 41, no. 3 [July 1989]: 378) pays special attention to the Orthodox contribution to this unity formula and refers to the important article by Nikos Nissiotis, "The Witness and the Service of Eastern Orthodoxy to the One Undivided Church," in *The Orthodox Church in the Ecumenical Movement*, ed. C. Patelos (Geneva: WCC, 1978), 231ff.

107. Lukas Vischer, ed., *Spirit of God, Spirit of Christ: Ecumenical Reflections on the Filioque Controversy* (London: SPCK/Geneva: WCC, 1981), 18.

108. "The Healing Mission of the Church," no. 37, Commission for World Mission and Evangelization, World Council of Churches, preparatory paper no. 11 for the May 2005 CWME Conference in Athens, "Come Holy Spirit, Heal and Reconcile—Called in Christ to Be Reconciling and Healing Communities," http://www.mission2005.org. Also available at http://www.oikoumene.org/en/resources/documents/wcc-commissions/mission-and-evangelism/cwme-world-conference-athens-2005/preparatory-paper-n-11-the-healing-mission-of-the-church.html.

109. Ibid., 40.

110. "Religious Plurality and Christian Self-Understanding," # 32, 33 (San Antonio: CWME, 1989), http://www.wcc-coe.org/wcc/what/interreligious/cd45-02.html.

111. A. Johnson, *She Who Is: The Mystery of God in Feminist Theological Discourse* (New York: Crossroad, 1992), 136.

112. Victoria B. Demarest, *Sex and Spirit: God, Woman and Ministry* (St. Petersburg: Sacred Arts Int'l, 1977), 38–39.

113. Anne Fatula, OP, *The Holy Spirit: Unbounded Gift of Joy* (Collegeville, MN: Liturgical Press, 1998), 2, 5, 22.

114. Rosemary R. Ruether, *Goddesses and the Divine Feminine: A Wisdom Religious History* (Berkeley: University of California Press, 2005), 132.

115. Johnson, *She Who Is*, 1.

116. Catherine Mowry LaCugna, *God for Us: The Trinity and Christian Life* (San Francisco: HarperSanFrancisco, 1993), 362.

117. Elizabeth Johnson, *Women, Earth and Creator Spirit* (Mahwah, NJ: Paulist Press, 1993), 42.

118. Ibid., 43.

119. Mark I. Wallace, *Fragments of the Spirit: Nature, Violence, and the Renewal of Creation* (New York: Continuum, 1996).

120. Mark I. Wallace, *Finding God in the Singing River* (Minneapolis: Augsburg Fortress, 2005), 6, 8, respectively.

121. Geiko Müller-Fahrenholz, *God's Spirit: Transforming a World in Crisis*, trans. John Cumming (New York: Continuum, 1995).

122. Miroslav Volf, *Work in the Spirit: Toward a Theology of Work* (Eugene, OR: Wipf & Stock, 2001).

123. John Polkinghorne, "The Hidden Spirit and the Cosmos," in *The Work of the Spirit: Pneumatology and Pentecostalism*, ed. Michael Welker (Grand Rapids: Wm. B. Eerdmans Publishing Co., 2006), 171.

124. Almir C. Bruneti, "The Feast of the Holy Spirit," Tulane University Latin American Library, http://lal.tulane.edu/programs/exhibits/feast.htm.

125. See further, William Dyrness, *Learning about Theology from the Third World* (Grand Rapids: Zondervan, 1990), 71–72.

126. José Comblin, *The Holy Spirit and Liberation*, trans. Paul Burns (Maryknoll, NY: Orbis Books, 1989), xi.
127. Jon Sobrino, *Spirituality of Liberation: Toward Political Holiness* (Maryknoll, NY: Orbis Books, 1988), 49.
128. Comblin, *Holy Spirit and Liberation*, 94–95, 99.
129. Daniel Chiquete, "Healing, Salvation, and Mission: The Ministry of Healing in Latin American Pentecostalism," *International Review of Mission*, 93, nos. 370–71 (2004): 479.
130. John S. Mbiti, *African Religions and Philosophy* (London: Heinemann, 1969), 2.
131. Tokunboh Adeyemo, "Unapproachable God: The High God of African Traditional Religion," in *The Global God: Multicultural Evangelical Views of God*, ed. Aida Besancon Spencer and William David Spencer (Grand Rapids: Baker, 1998), 130–31.
132. Osadolor Imasogie, *Guidelines for Christian Theology in Africa* (Achimota, Ghana: Africa Christian Press, 1993), 81.
133. Gwinyai H. Muzorewa, *The Origins and Development of African Theology* (Maryknoll, NY: Orbis Books, 1985), 84.
134. Imasogie, *Guidelines*, 81.
135. Ibid.
136. See Kwame Bediako, *Christianity in Africa: The Renewal of a Non-Western Religion* (Edinburgh: Edinburgh University Press, 1995), 176.
137. Donald J. Goergen, OP, "The Quest for the Christ of Africa," *African Christian Studies* 17, no. 1 (March 2001), http://www.sedos.org/english/goergen.htm.
138. H. W. Turner, *Religious Innovation in Africa* (Boston: G. K. Hall, 1979), 210.
139. Citing from Paul Tillich, *The Eternal Now* (New York: Charles Scribner's Sons, 1963), 83–84.
140. Caleb Oluremi Oladipo, *The Development of the Doctrine of the Holy Spirit in the Yoruba (African) Indigenous Christian Movement*, American University Studies, series 2, Theology and Religion, vol. 185 (Frankfurt: Peter Lang, 1996), 100.
141. Ibid., 104, 107.
142. Aloysius Pieris, "Western Christianity and Asian Buddhism," *Dialogue* 7 (May–August 1980): 61–62.
143. Yeow Choo Lak, preface to *Doing Theology with the Spirit's Movement in Asia*, ed. John C. England and Alan J. Torrance (Singapore: ATESEA, 1991), vi.
144. Jung Young Lee, *The Theology of Change: A Christian Concept of God in an Eastern Perspective* (Maryknoll, NY: Orbis Books, 1979), 110.
145. Jung Young Lee, *The Trinity in Asian Perspective* (Nashville: Abingdon Press, 1996), 95.
146. Ibid., 95–96.
147. Kirsteen Kim, *The Holy Spirit in the World: A Global Conversation* (Maryknoll, NY: Orbis Books, 2007), 181.
148. Stanley J. Samartha, *Between Two Cultures: Ecumenical Ministry in a Pluralist World* (Geneva: WCC Publications, 1996), 187.
149. Stanley J. Samartha, *Courage for Dialogue: Ecumenical Issues in Inter-Religious Relationships* (Geneva: WCC Publications, 1981), 76.
150. "The Spirit at Work in Asia Today: A Document of the Office of Theological Concerns of the Federation of the Asian Bishops' Conferences," FABC Papers no. 81 (1998), 1–2.

Postscript

1. Lesslie Newbigin, *Unfinished Agenda: An Autobiography* (Grand Rapids: Wm. B. Eerdmans Publishing Co., 1985).

For Further Reading

Anderson, Allan H. *Moya: The Holy Spirit from an African Perspective.* Pretoria: University of South Africa, 1994.

Badcock, Gary D. *Light of Truth and Fire of Love: A Theology of the Holy Spirit.* Grand Rapids: Wm. B. Eerdmans Publishing Co., 1997.

Burgess, Stanley M. *The Holy Spirit: Ancient Christian Traditions.* Peabody, MA: Hendrickson, 1984.

———. *The Holy Spirit: Eastern Christian Traditions.* Peabody, MA: Hendrickson, 1989.

———. *The Holy Spirit: Medieval Roman Catholic and Reformation Traditions.* Peabody, MA: Hendrickson, 1997.

Congar, Yves. *I Believe in the Holy Spirit* (three volumes in one). New York: Herder, 1997.

Del Colle, R. *Christ and the Spirit: Spirit Christology in Trinitarian Perspective.* Oxford: Oxford University Press 1994.

Fee, Gordon. *God's Empowering Presence: The Holy Spirit in the Letters of Paul.* Peabody, MA: Hendrickson, 1994.

Gomblin, J. *The Holy Spirit and Liberation.* Maryknoll, NY: Orbis, 1989.

Johnson, Elizabeth. *She Who Is: The Mystery of God in Feminist Theological Discourse.* New York: Crossroad, 1992.

Kim, Kirsteen. *The Holy Spirit in the World: A Global Conversation.* Maryknoll, NY: Orbis, 2007.

Kärkkäinen, Veli-Matti. *Pneumatology: The Holy Spirit in Ecumenical, International, and Contextual Perspectives.* Grand Rapids: Baker Academic, 2002.

Lossky, Vladimir. *The Mystical Theology of the Eastern Church.* Crestwood, NY: St. Vladimir's Seminary Press, 1998.

Macchia, Frank. *Baptized in the Spirit: A Global Pentecostal Theology.* Grand Rapids: Zondervan, 2006.

Moltmann, Jürgen. *The Spirit of Life: A Universal Affirmation.* Translated by Margaret Kohl. Minneapolis: Fortress Press, 1994.

Montague, George. *The Holy Spirit: Growth of a Biblical Tradition.* Peabody, MA: Hendrickson, 1994.

Müller-Fahrenholz, Geiko. *God's Spirit: Transforming a World in Crisis.* New York: Continuum, 1995.

Pinnock, Clark H. *Flame of Love: A Theology of the Holy Spirit.* Downers Grove, IL: InterVarsity Press, 1996.

Prichard, Rebecca Button. *Sensing the Spirit: The Holy Spirit in Feminist Perspective.* St. Louis: Chalice Press, 1999.

Shults, F. Leron, and Andrea Hollingsworth. *The Holy Spirit.* Guides to Theology. Grand Rapids: Wm. B. Eerdmans Publishing Co., 2008.

Welker, M. *God the Spirit.* Minneapolis: Fortress Press, 1992.

Yong, Amos. *The Spirit Poured Out on All Flesh: Pentecostalism and the Possibility of Global Theology.* Grand Rapids: Baker Academic, 2005.

Index

LaCugna, Catherine Mowry, 96
Lampe, Geoffrey, 84
Latin American interpretations, 76, 98–99
Lee, Jung Young, 101
Lee, Paul D., 93
lex orandi lex crendendi (the law of prayer [is or becomes] the law of believing), 10, 16, 19, 47. *See also* doxology, including the Spirit
Liberation theologies. *See* Latin American interpretations
Lossky, Vladimir, 78
"love" or "bond of love," Spirit as, 2, 23–24, 30, 41, 73
Luther, Martin, 45–52

Magisterial Reformers, 45–53
Maximus the Confessor, 32
Mbiti, John, 99
McDonnell, Kilian, 82
Melanchthon, Philipp, 51
metaphors and symbols for the Spirit, 5, 8, 15, 23, 31, 35, 37–38, 47, 54–55, 67, 96, 100–101, 110n69
  arrabon (down payment), 7
  flame, 35, 53–55
  fountain and river, 15, 20
  kiss, 36, 38
  light, beam of the sun, 12, 15, 20, 67
  living water, 34, 55
  mother, 57, 101
  two hands of God, 14, 82–83
  See also "love" or bond of "love," Spirit as; Paraclete; *ruach*; wisdom, Sophia, Spirit as
miracles, 6, 22, 42–43, 64, 73
mission of Church, missionary impetus, 76–77, 80, 88, 93, 99, 101
modalist, modalism, 13, 15, 83–84
Moltmann, Jürgen, 85–88
Montanists, 2, 13, 17
Müller-Fahrenholz, Geiko, 97
Müntzer, Thomas, 50, 55
mutuality and equality of trinitarian persons, 24–25, 42, 85–86, 89. See also *perichoresis*
mystical and ecstatic experiences, 12, 29, 35–37, 43, 54–55, 63, 66, 76

nature of the Holy Spirit, 21, 40–42, 73
Neo-Calvinist School, 70–72

new birth, 62–63, 67
New Testament, 6–8, 11, 20, 28, 30, 50, 89, 100. *See also* Paul, Pauline literature
Nicea. *See* creedal statements, Holy Spirit in
nineteenth-century theologies, 68–73

Old Testament, 5–6, 23, 28
Oluremi, Caleb, 100
one/same substance, "one substance in three persons" (*una substantia, tres personae*), 15, 24
ordo salutis, 58–59, 67, 70, 87, 89–90
Origen, 14–15, 17, 109n44
Owen, John, 60–61

panentheist, 86–87
Pannenberg, Wolfhart, 88–90, 104
Paraclete, 5, 7, 15, 47, 79
Paul, Pauline literature, 7, 20, 34, 54, 56, 60, 65, 98–99
Penn, William, 67
Pentecost, 6, 43, 66
  hymn for 43–44
pentecostal and charismatic movements (20th c.), 73, 75–77, 98–100
perfection, Christian, 64–65
perichoresis (inner-Trinitarian), 25
Perpetua and Felicitas, passion of, 13
Peter Abelard, 43
Pieris, Aloysius, 101
Pietism, 62–64
Pinnock, Clark H., 91–92
Polkinghorne, John, 97
preacher, preaching, 12, 25, 35–36, 47, 49–50, 60–63, 65, 67–68, 83
Princeton orthodoxy. *See* Reformed (Princeton) orthodoxy
Priscilla and Maximilla, 13
procession, 30, 41–42. *See also* filioque
prophet, prophecy, 13, 17, 36–37, 43
Puritanism, 59–62

Quakers, 66–67

Radical Reformers, 45, 49–50, 55–56
Rahner, Karl, 81–82
Reformed (Princeton) orthodoxy, 72–73
resurrection of Jesus by the Spirit, 7, 61, 97

CPSIA information can be obtained
at www.ICGtesting.com
Printed in the USA
LVHW040301060819
626610LV00004B/11

9 780664 235932